D1057340

WHERE HAVE ALL THE MOTHERS GONE?

Brenda Hunter

Zondervan Publishing House
Grand Rapids, Michigan

WHERE HAVE ALL THE MOTHERS GONE?

Zondervan Publishing House,
1415 Lake Drive, S.E.,
Grand Rapids, Michigan 49506

LIBRARY OF CONGRESS CATALOGING IN PUBLICATION DATA

Hunter, Brenda.
Where have all the mothers gone?

1. Mothers—United States. 2. Mother and child—United States. 3. Mothers—Employment—United States. 4. Parenting—Religious aspects—Christianity. I. Title.

HQ759.H85 1982 649′.1 82-13707
ISBN 0-310-45550-2

Edited by Betsy Stine and Judith E. Markham
Designed by Louise Bauer

Printed in the United States of America

84 85 86 87 88 89 90 — 12 11 10 9 8 7 6 5 4

Contents

To my husband
Don,
whose love and daily encouragement
have called forth my gifts.

Introduction

This book is about mothers and their children—more specifically the painful dilemma many mothers face in the eighties as they attempt to define their personal worth and at the same time parent their children.

While the mothering role has always been demanding, until some twenty years ago the value and status of motherhood was unassailable. Today this is not the case. Numerous feminists, in their militant crusade for equality of the sexes, have disparaged children and the place they have traditionally occupied in a woman's life and psyche. As women have been encouraged to leave home for the marketplace, earn higher salaries, and find fulfillment and identity in their work, the role of mothering has been progressively devalued. Now some women even apologize for believing that they, and not a day-care center, are best suited to rear their children.

As a result many women find themselves caught in a tremendous bind. On the one hand, they have their biological need to mother, their psychological imperative to nurture, and an age-old identity based on these activities. On the other hand, they have a very understandable drive for status and affirmation. And the culture is issuing no plaudits to the women who opt for motherhood at the expense of a full-time career.

This conflict in values is reflected in the way women feel. While the full-time working mother may feel good about her career, she feels guilty about her children. She has rationalized her absence from their lives, but she is not at peace. The mother who stays home is also torn. She feels guilty because she is not working and fears she may indeed be wasting her life and her gifts by remaining at home with her children.

And few of the mothers I have talked to, whether they work outside the home or not, believe they are close to finding that elusive fulfillment that they have been told is their birthright.

Is this the way we are to live our lives—riven by conflicts and myriad self-doubts? I do not believe so. God would have us live meaningful, productive, guilt-free lives. Out of my own struggle I have written this book for those mothers who want to take a fresh look at themselves, their children, their culture, who want to resolve this dilemma, who want to feel good about mothering.

REFLECTIONS OF A FORMER FEMINIST

1

Where Are All Those Warm, Surrogate Mothers?

> Children are the anchors that hold a mother to life.
> Sophocles

My own views on the importance of mothering have changed dramatically since my children were born. During my twenties when I was married to a physician in training and having my babies, I was quite willing for someone else to help in the child-rearing process. Having read Betty Friedan's *The Feminine Mystique* when my first child was about nine months old, I felt I had found—at last—an explanation for my attitudes toward my life. Now I knew why I felt an inner restlessness when I was home alone with my baby. I was an educated woman who was literally wasting her mind and her life. The answer? To resume college teaching and pick up the threads of a career that existed before Holly was born.

It helped that my husband, then an intern at a prestigious teaching hospital, made only four thousand dollars yearly. We could barely live on his salary, so both of us were grateful when I found a full-time teaching position at a nearby college. Even if we had not needed the money, I would have gone back to work. I loved college teaching, and Thomas and I had already discovered that the best antidote for my inner restlessness was a job.

I soon learned, however, that I could no longer pursue a career with an unfettered mind. As I drove off in the morning, leaving Holly with the sitter, I found it hard to forget about her and turn all my energies in the direction of work. I worried about her development and the quality of care she would receive in my absence. Only with great effort was I able to push her image out of my mind and concentrate on my work and personal fulfillment.

I told myself as I drove the fifteen miles to the college that I was different from those stay-at-home mothers who lost themselves in coffee klatsches and silly games with their babies. I needed to be productive and do something useful with my life. Certainly raising a child was productive and could give me feelings of usefulness, but I believed I could interact sufficiently with Holly before and after work. I loved her dearly—she was my first baby, a beautiful little girl—but I needed intellectual stimulation and the feeling that my life counted for something. Besides, my husband Thomas was seldom there physically (he had a demanding on-call schedule); and when he was at home, he was so exhausted that he had little to give. In truth, Holly and I led emotionally impoverished lives in this new location until I made friendships through my work.

So while I spent my days teaching literature and freshman writing, Holly stayed in a mobile home with another mother and child. I do not know how Holly spent her days; I can only assume the sitter told me the truth and that she gave Holly adequate care. But while Holly's days were a blank to me, my days were full and rewarding. I enjoyed my work immensely, and my students affirmed me most of the time. Moreover, I had excellent rapport with my colleagues and grew intellectually from this experience.

In addition, the salary I earned financed lunches out with friends, lovely clothes, and vacations with Thomas. No longer was I an intern's depressed wife, mother of one child, who had little to say when the other doctors' wives asked that powerful question: "What do you do?" Instead, as a college instructor, I had status among the other interns and their wives, and this was no small sop for any anxiety I felt about Holly.

All went well until I had to change sitters after three months. As I searched for another caretaker for Holly, I looked for a woman who would come to our apartment, care for my child, clean, and iron those impossible starched white uniforms that Thomas wore daily. I felt that it would be better for Holly to stay in her own environment, and it would certainly be more convenient for me.

This second arrangement worked for three months. Each day when I returned home, Holly was sitting on the sitter's lap, immaculate, fingering a small toy. The apartment shone, and Thomas's uniforms hung neatly in a row. I soon learned, however, that Holly was spending long hours penned up in her crib while the caretaker ironed those uniforms and rendered my home immaculate. I was appalled. A follower of all the latest theories on child development, I had always allowed Holly to roam our apartment freely. What, I wondered, would be the effect upon my child of all those hours spent imprisoned in her crib?

Distressed, I told the sitter that she would have to leave and I undertook the arduous task of working full-time while trying to find the third caretaker in six months for my lovely first-born. I needed to find that warm, surrogate mother I had read about, that sterling woman who would make a significant commitment to my child and at the same time rear her according to my standards. I finally found a modified version of this Wonderful Surrogate Mother, caring for eight other children in her plain, small bungalow. Word traveled among the interns' wives that a Duke University psychologist had observed Mrs. York's interaction with her charges and had given her a first-class rating. So Holly became the ninth child who regularly visited Mrs. York's home and vied for her attention.

What a relief to find a stable situation at last. Holly remained with Mrs. York for the duration of Thomas's internship and until we moved north for his residency. She proved to be a steady if subdued caretaker. The only thing that gave me pause was the fact that I found Mrs. York mopping her kitchen floor most afternoons while her tired charges waited just beyond the wooden gate that separated her from them. Although Mrs. York turned her whole house into a nursery school for most of the day, when the afternoon waned she mopped with a concentration that amazed me while fussy babies and toddlers chorused in the adjoining room. But all the other mothers seemed to have no qualms, and the children were too young to discuss their day, so my guilt was soothed.

One fact became increasingly clear, however, as I went through the process of leaving my small daughter. While I as educated middle-class mother might be conversant with the latest child development theories and hold definite views about how I wished Holly to be raised, from the moment I dropped her off at the sitter's I had no idea how she spent her time. I did not know what she did during the hours I worked and enjoyed lunches with colleagues. Did she spend those hours in a playpen, crib, or highchair, or all three? Were her diapers changed regularly? Did the sitter respond to the signals my baby gave when she needed stimulation or cuddling? Did she have an opportunity to try her new skill of walking or was she penned up far too long? Did the sitter treat her with tenderness or did she handle her roughly because she had so many babies to feed and change?

And how did this Wonderful Surrogate Mother feel about my child? Although I felt I had other tasks that demanded my attention, I wished to employ someone who would consider the care of my child a primary responsibility. Moreover, I wanted this woman to find caring for my baby fulfilling in a way I had not (I did not consider the irony of this at all) and at the same time combine the qualities of earth mother with those of child-development expert. Finally, I wanted this woman to love children—mine in particular—and know what they needed in terms of love and care. I thought little of the fact that she could not possibly attend to the signals of nine small children at once. In the area of mothering, I clearly expected more of Mrs. York than I expected of myself.

All of these concerns were either unspoken or unconscious. Never did I ask Mrs. York if she loved children or if she chose to care for them because of her overwhelming concern for their needs. Nor did I ever query her about her views on child-rearing or about the quality of mothering she had received. Like many other mothers I know, I looked for someone who was personable and warm. Not inconsequential was the fact that Mrs. York was *willing* to care for Holly. Perhaps I did not ask too many questions or probe too deeply because had I done so, I would not have been able to leave Holly and go happily off to work.

When my second child, another daughter, arrived, my husband was a resident in psychiatry earning seven thousand dollars yearly. We purchased a home far from Thomas's work, and I tried staying home with two children under two and a half. Logistically, it was harder to find someone to care for the two babies. We had little spendable cash, and for a while we owned only one car which Thomas drove thirty miles to work. If I wanted the car for the day, I had to drive Thomas to work with two babies in tow and then return in rush-hour traffic to pick him up. The round trips equaled 120 miles a day. Most days I was home alone in suburbia, increasingly aware of marital estrangement, trapped in our house. In a short time I became depressed.

Both Thomas and I decided that I needed to go back to work, so we went in debt for a second car and I found a part-time position at a local college. Holly then went to her fourth sitter and Kristen, who was eight months old, to her first. Although the job relieved some of my inner angst, we barely broke even financially.

As life would have it, this arrangement lasted briefly. My frequently absent and withdrawn husband soon found someone else at the medical center where he was in training and ultimately left me to marry her. (I have written of this most wrenching experience in my first book, *Beyond Divorce*). Suffice it to say that very quickly I went from being a married woman whose work supplemented her husband's income to being a single parent who felt she had to work. The money that Thomas agreed to give me did not even fund our basic needs.

So I located a full-time teaching position at a high school miles away and farmed out the children in earnest. Now for the first time ever I was really banking on that Wonderful Surrogate Mother to come through for the children since I, depressed and harried, had little to give them.

During the year after Thomas left, I was fortunate in finding a woman who grew fond of both girls, especially Kristen. So close did the bond between Mrs. McCarthy and Kristen become that one day my baby whimpered and turned from me when she had to leave the sitter's arms for mine. That hurt. Kristen was only twenty months old and already she and I were losing touch with each other.

After that first horrendous year alone, I felt the children and I desperately needed a change in lifestyle. I discovered that being a separated mother in suburbia was a particular kind of lonely hell. The children and I were isolated from any meaningful human interchange. I developed few ties with coworkers, and the neighbors stayed safely away, apparently not wishing to involve themselves in anything as messy as a broken marriage. Believing that I must find a more human lifestyle, I sold most of our possessions, resigned from my job, and moved the three of us across the Atlantic to England to participate in the life of a Christian community.

During the two years I lived in London and participated in the nourishing life of a small supportive community called L'Abri Fellowship, I stayed home with the girls and discovered to my absolute surprise that I did not get depressed. Not only did our new friends include us in holiday festivities, but I now had other adults to interact with during the day. Moreover, the children had people who were interested in them and included them in meals and outings. Consequently, all three of us had our inner lives mended as we were loved and cared for in practical ways.

After two years with this supportive community—time when I reestablished loving bonds with the children and clarified my ideas about child-rearing—we moved to the West Coast. I prepared to go back to work. While Thomas's modest support check had funded our lifestyle in England (this was before England joined the Common Market and inflation hit), it would not cover our needs in America.

As I searched for work this time, however, things were different because I was different inside. No longer was I looking for a job to quell the inner restlessness. That restlessness was simply gone. Those two years in England had changed my view of myself and my children. I had found a new perspective on my life in biblical Christianity. I now saw that my children, who had always been loved, were a top priority and a high responsibility. They were, as it says in Psalm 127, a "gift from the Lord." More than ever before, I was ready to deepen my commitment to them and consider their welfare before my own. Because I internalized so much love from these Christians at the L'Abri Fellowship, I could now give my young children what they needed, without that restless preoccupation with self-fulfillment which had haunted me earlier.

Believing that my daughters, then four and six, needed my attention for part of each day, I searched for part-time work and, through the encouragement of a lawyer who was also a Christian, started my own business as an editorial consultant. This afforded flexibility and enabled me to earn a reasonable hourly fee which, when I added it up, paid better than teaching. I thus needed to work only four hours each day and occasional evenings after the girls had gone to bed.

Still requiring some daily child-care for Kristen, I began the round of day-care facilities in the suburb where we lived. When I finally located a day-care center which was acceptable—one that was clean, well-equipped, and staffed with professional teachers—I was pleased to find it near our home. Kristen had a sunny teacher who had formerly taught music in an elementary school. Mrs. James was warm, attractive, and poised, and I felt confidence in her as a person and as a teacher. Because she was so competent, however, she did not remain at the center long but left for better opportunities.

When Mrs. James left, Kristen, who is an articulate child, let me know in no uncertain terms that she did not wish to go to the day-care center any longer. Not only did she miss her teacher, but Kris, who had long since given up her nap, now had to lie on her cot for a long rest period. Bored, Kristen begged me to stay home so that she could also. Even after I spoke to the supervisor and secured crayons and paper for her to use during the rest periods, Kristen did not relish her days at the center. She was never happier than when I arrived in early afternoon to pick her up; then she sang and chatted happily all the way home.

Kristen and I had numerous conversations about my working. She made it quite clear that she wanted to stay in our little house and play with her toys and nearby friends. And she stated unequivocably that she wanted more of my mother-presence. She longed to be home, for she disliked the regimentation of the day-care center which ignored her developmental schedule. Though she went each day without argument, both she and I understood just how she felt.

One painful memory remains from all those days of day-care. Whenever I dropped Kristen off on warm days, she would hurriedly kiss me good-by and rush past all her acquaintances to the enclosed play area. Once inside the gate, she flew to the fence, clambered up, and waved to me until I was out of sight. As I drove off to work, I could see Kristen's determined little face in my rear view mirror and, knowing she would rather be home with me, I felt a wrenching inside. That sad little ritual, captured in memory, tugged at all my mother feelings. It was hard to leave her, even for a short time.

I left my children for good reasons. Initially, I was unhappy at home and believed sincerely that they would not be hurt as I pursued personal fulfillment through my teaching career. And when my first marriage ended, I worked full-time because I felt I had no other option.

Beginning with the time at L'Abri, my life has changed. I have changed inside and have come to some conclusions that would cause me to live those years differently. I now believe that God will augment our limited funds if we have the right priorities, and our children are certainly a top priority in any mother's life. And I know that no mother who is a believer need wither in loneliness and isolation.

From years of growing, reading, and listening to my children, I have come to see just how much I contribute to their feelings of security and well-being. As I have understood my enormous value in their lives, God has deepened my love and concern for them until I now consider child-rearing the most significant work I do.

Rearing my daughters well—teaching them about God, communicating academic knowledge as well as coping strategies, and binding up their wounds—this is where much of my energy is going. Speaking engagements, writing, and occasional television appearances are stimulating and provide creative outlets, yet my children's emotional well-being outweighs any accomplishments.

That is why I am now, at forty-one, unwilling to pursue a full-time career outside the home. Although child care authorities say Holly and Kristen are old enough to be independent and alone for most of their waking hours, I wish to be physically and emotionally present during the hours before and after school. Some mornings I reassure a nervous child that she will perform well on that standardized test; other mornings I am just there as mother. And when Kristen rushes home from school for what she calls "the best part of my day," I am there to listen as she recounts her day. When Holly pokes her blond head inside the door or stands in the kitchen munching on a snack, I take time to enjoy my elder daughter.

Why is it important that I am present before and after school? My children need me to provide mother-solace when they have been wounded; they need my affirmation as they build self-esteem; they need love as exemplified by my interested presence because the world can be cold and forbidding on occasion.

Like other mothers of school-age children, I have all the hours when the girls are away to work and be creative. Those are the times to write books, teach seminars, speak to women's groups. But when they come through the door after school, it is then time to pack the typewriter away, listen, savor a cup of tea, and experience unhurried time with my children.

2

"Lonely As a Cloud"

I wandered lonely as a cloud
That floats on high o'er vales and hills
William Wordsworth

WHEN I LOOK back into my childhood, and relive in memory events that surface, the predominant feeling that emerges is loneliness. Except for visits to my grandfather's farm and to the homes of a few other relatives, I grew up basically alone.

My mother was unable to stay home when I was a young child. My father, a college junior when he married, drowned when I was two years old and my sister a mere two months. Since he left only five hundred dollars in life insurance, my mother sought and found full-time employment within a year after his death. Believing that she could not rear two small children and work full-time, she left me with my paternal grandparents and moved to a nearby town with my sister, Sandy. I was a vulnerable three-year-old at that time.

No sooner had I begun to transfer love to my grandparents, particularly my grandfather, when mother appeared and asked my middle-aged grandmother to switch children. Later when I asked Granny about this sad event, she who was then in her eighties remarked, "It was one of the hardest things I ever did. Just when we had started to think of you as our very own child, I had to give you up and start all over again with Sandy. Oh, I loved Sandy, too, but when your mother took you away, so soon after the death of your father, it nearly broke my heart."

It was not that mother was insensitive to feelings. She was worried about Sandy and felt she was too young to spend her days with sitters. A negligent sitter had allowed Sandy to burn herself on their wood stove and this event prompted mother to exchange the children. I was at least older and at four could articulate my feelings. Thus, my sister and I were traded and raised as "lonely, only children," she on a dairy farm and I in a small southern town.

Although my mother tried to find sitters to stay with me while she worked, from about the age of seven on I often came home from school to an empty apartment. Even now I remember distinctly the cold fear that enveloped me as I unlocked the front door and entered the darkened apartment. What if a burglar lurked in the dim recesses of a closet or under the bed? On those days I made a hurried examination of the premises before my body slowly relaxed.

But even on the days when no fear stalked me, I disliked returning home to our empty apartment. No matter how sunny the weather outside, no matter how warm the air, the atmosphere of our empty home was dark and forbidding. No human voice rang out to dispel the gloom, assuring me that it was safe to enter. No mother arms reached out to give a welcoming hug. And if I had been wounded by a teacher or another child, and came home needing attention? That need to have my self-esteem buttressed had to be ignored. Or if the day brought joy in the form of a good grade or praise? No mother was there to share in the good feelings.

Even though mother telephoned to inquire about my day, her call did not make me feel suddenly warmed and loved. Her arms could not come through the telephone wires to encircle me, and I knew she was busy. Preoccupied with work, she tried to reach out to me, but at the same time she desired the call to end so that she could get back to work. I knew my needs had to be contained; so in time I learned to communicate superficially, hitting only the highlights of the day.

Since mother had not finished high school, she had few employment opportunities and worked as a telephone operator for most of the years of my childhood. Sometimes her job required that she work split shifts. When this occurred, mother often walked the three miles round-trip in order to spend part of her day with me. I knew she was trying to be a good mother, and so I accepted my life's aloneness.

How I dreaded those evenings when mother worked late. I either had to heat up something she had cooked earlier or walk across the field to an unpainted house where a silent neighbor provided dinner. Sitting alone at a table (I never ate with the family), I ate simple fare: vegetables, biscuits, and a concoction called pan gravy which was served over a slice of bread. I do not know what mother paid this woman, but the meal served in silence nourished neither body nor spirit.

After supper on those evenings, I walked home alone. Our three-room apartment was built caboose fashion with a living room, bedroom, and kitchen strung in a row. On the back porch was a tiny room that housed a toilet. On those nights when I was home alone, I turned on every light in our apartment and positioned myself in the middle of the living room floor so that I could look through to the back porch. Trying to read, yet unable to concentrate, I prayed that no burglar would come, since on those summer nights only a latch on the back and front screen doors separated me from the world of darkness beyond all light. How terrifying and lonely those nights were.

When mother worked days, I became a street child, playing with the children up the road or riding the neighbor boy's bike down a steep hill. Companionship, noise, color, light were "out there" away from our empty apartment. So I fled our apartment whenever life afforded an opportunity. Although my world outside was small at first, consisting of a few nearby yards and the blocks between the apartment and the grammar school, as I grew older my world grew larger. By the time I reached fifth grade, I had crisscrossed the entire town many times on foot.

Like millions of other children, I accepted the fact that my mother worked. How else, she often stated, would we live? And to my mother, working meant full-time employment. Her job, coupled with child-care, took most of her energies.

Mother strained to rear a child alone, earn a meager income, and deal with her own needs for companionship as a single parent still in her twenties. She found the going rough and was often tired, irritable, or simply preoccupied. I preferred her irritability to her preoccupation. At least then she became involved with me.

Because her energies were going toward maintaining an apartment and working, mother did not effectively discipline her headstrong daughter. I knew that if I pressed my tired mother long enough, she would usually capitulate. Occasionally I overstepped the bounds and mother came running after me with a hair brush. But for the most part her attempts at discipline were abortive, and I, consequently, grew up with little respect for authority.

Nor did mother have the energy or the desire to provide the intellectual stimulation I needed. Having grown up in poverty in what was essentially a motherless home, mother had little concept of stretching a child's mind. Occasionally she read popular novels on loan from a neighbor, which she retold to me, expurgating the erotic passages as she went along. This gave some color to our life together, especially when mother moved on to tell stories from her own childhood and adolescence.

Not surprisingly, I became a gregarious child who had abundant friendships to flesh out an otherwise impoverished life. Not only did these young girls provide companionship and fill up many after-school hours, but, best of all, most had mothers at home. My favorite days occurred when I did not go home to our empty apartment but went instead to a home where a mother waited.

In memory those days stand out in bold relief. They provided a keen contrast to life at home. Compared to my frequently harried, intense mother, these women who had husbands to support them seemed almost carefree. Of course, they weren't, but neither were they alone in the child-rearing process.

Those stay-at-home mothers profoundly influenced my young life. One, who was pregnant with her third child, allowed me to feel her swollen abdomen and taught me about the joy of childbirth. Another, a fine pianist, not only filled my untutored ears with the sound of classical music but she and her daughter were emotionally close. As I watched their interaction, I saw an intimacy that my mother and I did not share, and this mother-daughter relationship touched a longing too deep for words.

When I became an adolescent, another neighbor introduced me to Christianity. Martha was a follower of Jesus, a Jesus so real that He paid her rent and food bill when her husband, an alcoholic, disappeared for periods of time. As I watched this strong, joyful woman rise above the wretchedness of her circumstances, I too wanted to know this Jesus. Gradually He became a reality to me, and in the process I became Martha's "child of the spirit," or so she called me.

These mothers who were present both physically and emotionally for their young daughters probably did not realize that they were, in some sense, mothering me. How grateful I am that they were there, bright oases dotting the desert of my life. How empty my days would have been if they, too, had been working and their daughters and I had simply played together in empty houses.

In addition to friends and their mothers, I did have paternal grandparents who provided love and companionship. My visits with them and my sister, Sandy, were the golden moments of my childhood. When I stepped off the bus to grasp grandaddy's hand and walk up the country lane to the farm, I was happy. Quietly, deeply happy. Here was no empty house, no fear, no coldness. The farmhouse was *alive* with people. In addition to grandparents and Sandy, my boon companion, both an unmarried aunt and uncle still lived at home. The house rang with the sound of human voices, and the smells of delicious farm cooking wafted from the kitchen.

For a child used to biscuits and beans eaten alone, granny's food was extraordinary. She baked two different kinds of pie daily, fried golden chicken, and made apple dumplings frequently. Known far and wide as a good cook, granny often had guests appear at mealtimes. Grandaddy's cronies knew where they could find good food and southern hospitality.

Better than food, however, was the fact that my grandparents were always there. Granny could be found somewhere in house or garden, and grandaddy was either in the barn or field. How wonderful to wander over field or meadow and know that a caring adult was never far away. How safe this felt.

As we brought in the cows and milked them in the barn, grandaddy took every opportunity to stretch my young mind. He taught me about the Depression when he had worked for fifty cents a day and was grateful for the money, about politics and the Democrats who alone could lead America, and about his courtship of granny. On some rare occasions he spoke of wind and stars, truth and morality. While granny nourished my body and provided some maternal nurture, grandaddy nurtured my spirit and fed my soul.

When the day came to return home, I found it hard to leave all that warmth and laughter for lonely, boring days with a tired working mother. I turned to books to replace the living, breathing people on the farm. Instead of walks with grandaddy and the moments when we spoke of truth and deep feeling, I now had thousands of hours to read. Although I loved reading and still do, books were no substitute for missing parental companionship.

True, I did become independent. If mother works full-time and leaves her child alone for hours, her child will learn to live without her. Children can easily learn to unlock doors, prepare simple meals, turn on the television to block out aloneness. But they can also learn, as I did, to internalize both negative and positive feelings until it becomes difficult in the extreme to bare the inner self before another. The walls I built then did not come down until I was nearly thirty and life forced me to become more open. Those who urge mothers to seek fulfillment through a career and at the same time rear independent children fail to tell you that a child can be independent and still possess a lonely heart.

I was that child. Outwardly all seemed well: I made all A's on report cards, had abundant friends, was well-liked by both children and adults. No obvious candidate for the school psychologist, I would have scored well on any sociogram.

But I wandered through many days of those early years lonely to my very core. The universe was essentially a lonely place, and life was to be lived in shadow, interspersed with bright moments. Gradually the feeling emerged as a question: Did anyone really care? That feeling persisted into my twenties and only deepened when my first marriage ended. It did not abate until, as an adult, I returned to Christianity and encountered a God who understands those feelings of lovelessness and lack of personal worth.

It would be dishonest to imply that all those sad and empty feelings stemmed from the fact that mother worked. If she and I had experienced a warm and continuous relationship during the first five or six years of my life, perhaps I could have handled her absence better. Only when I did the research for this book on bonding and the mother's strategic importance to her young child did I begin to understand the origin of some of my own feelings of lostness and unlove.

The loss of father and then a year later of mother must have affected my young life deeply. Then when mother reentered my life, after I had transferred love and loyalty to my grandparents, and removed me to yet another life, not only did I experience a succession of caretakers (which the experts say is harmful to the child), but I started to learn that love was somehow connected to loss. To love someone deeply was eventually to lose that love object and experience incredible inner pain.

Whatever the psychic import of those early transferals of love, suffice it to say, I have never felt close to my mother. The people who evoke those fond, warm memories in my early childhood are my grandparents, particularly my grandfather. Nor is mother close to Sandy, the child she, in effect, gave away.

From our conversations, I am aware of the intense sorrow mother feels because her younger daughter views her as a distant aunt. It is as if mother never expected that granny would become Sandy's psychological parent and forge a close mother-daughter relationship with her. As for me, most of my life I have longed for an intimate relationship with my mother and have only recently come to accept the fact that this may never occur.

From some source, however, I did receive enough love to know what intimacy feels like and to recreate it with my children. Whether this gift came from early years with my father or from my grandparents, I know not. But this ability to be close did not eradicate all the early wounds or insure that I would make life choices that would enable me to be the mother my daughters needed.

As I wrote in the preceding chapter, in my twenties I was open to what has now become a strident cultural message: namely, that my fulfillment would come from a successful career rather than from relational closeness with my children. Without considering the validity of this message, I assumed that it was true and that my children would manage without my mother-presence.

Because of my early life, I now strongly identify with the children growing up in America who must come home to empty houses. I believe I may understand their plight better than their mothers who grew up in homes where they enjoyed a mother's presence before and after school. I am convinced that many mothers who allow their children to return home to an empty house have no earthly idea what this feels like. How can they *know*, unless they have experienced it, about the loneliness and fear that haunt their young children's lives? Because I felt these emotions, I empathize with "latch key" children and will not recreate this experience for my daughters.

And what about those infants whose successful career mothers are back at work when their babies are a scant four or six weeks old? Will these babies effectively bond with their tired and preoccupied mothers? And as they experience a succession of caretakers before they attend school, will any of them grow up, as I did, feeling that no one in the universe cares?

This book challenges these present cultural attitudes about mothers and their children which are basically injurious to both. It is imperative that we take a hard look at the popular view that denigrates mothering and undersells the needs of children. For if we adopt the popular view, we do so at significant peril and great psychological loss.

CURRENT IMAGES OF MOTHER

3

It's Hard To Be a Mother Today

> Women today have too many options and too many pressures. Sometimes I don't know how to live my life.
>
> a contemporary woman

IT'S DIFFICULT TO be a mother in America today. At every turn we are told how to exercise, diet, dress-for-success, find fulfillment in career, and share tasks equally with husbands. Additionally, we are encouraged to rear good children on minimal time. It is assumed that we want to look like either Jane Fonda or Joanne Woodward, and so that lean, firm look is publicized with a vengeance. We then listen to the billion-dollar cosmetic industry tell us how to achieve the beautiful face and the right, sexy scent.

Narcissism is the philosophy of the age. Articles and books tell us that our first responsibility is to ourselves. It is wrong to live for family or to allow mother-feelings to curtail the pursuit of self. Since our children may well mess up their lives or at best will simply grow up and leave home, it is unwise to invest too much time in them. Besides, we might turn into "moms" and cause our children to become superneurotic. Husbands? They, too, may fail us. The escalation of divorce supports the idea that "number oneism" is all that's left. If we do not look out for ourselves, we just may find ourselves old, divorced, unfulfilled, and unemployed.

These current ideas, as well as the reality of inflation, have sent millions of mothers to the marketplace. There, in the world of work, they are not only able to increase their family's goods, but they can insure against a lonely and useless middle age.

And what of the mother who chooses to stay home because she feels she is the best person to care for her children? While the career mother has society's approbation, the stay-at-home mother has society's pity and contempt. Her major task, the rearing of her children, has been devalued, and many look askance at any woman who finds joy in housewifery. In addition, modern labor-saving devices have drastically reduced the value of her contribution in maintaining the home. Consequently, the housewife often finds herself at home without the moral support of even her husband.

The February 1979 issue of *McCalls* states that the modern housewife is angry and defensive; she has experienced a painful loss of self-esteem and feels she must justify her decision to stay home to a hostile and unsympathetic world.

Though living radically different lives, both the working mother and the housewife must meet additional heavy expectations. They must not only stay young (eternally) and look beautiful, but they must be the sexually active mistress-wife. Sex is no longer a freely chosen act; it has become an absolute requirement. Magazines dictate sexual frequency, technique, and orgasmic result. Never mind that a woman might be tired after a day of child care or a day at the office: A wife must at all times be a scintillating sexual partner or she is less than a woman since in this day of noncommitment, some other woman may be waiting in the wings if the wife lets down even for a moment. Said an attractive woman who is married to an airline pilot, "You seldom see pilots' wives who are overweight. They know that their husbands work with young, attractive stewardesses who provide keen competition."

Housewives are also pressed to "leave home." Magazine articles encourage women to work at the same time they are rearing their children. Career and children do mix, and mix well, says the media. Case histories in the women's magazines tell us of women who manage full-time careers and at the same time are effective, caring mothers. Look at the late Margaret Mead, who raised an accomplished daughter while making a major contribution to the field of anthropology. Who would not wish to emulate a Margaret Mead or earn the salary of a Barbara Walters?

At the same time we hear women being encouraged to leave home, husbands, and children for the world of work, we also hear rumbles of something called the breakdown of the American family. This breakdown is graphically experienced by the divorced mother whose lot is the hardest of all.

The divorced mother often has no husband to support her or the children while she decides what she will do with her life. Unless her husband is in the statistical minority that regularly pays adequate child support, the divorced mother has the burden of supporting herself and her children, often on a meager salary. Torn between the demands of her children and her career, she parents alone, with occasional time off when the divorced father visits his children.

With the burden of work and the sometimes total responsibility for the care of her children, the separated and divorced mother also has her emotional needs to contend with. Emotionally unsupported and sometimes exploited by the men who move through her life, the divorced mother may experience a succession of broken relationships and pain.

While she puts her life back together, the culture clearly tells her what is expected: She is to be a sexual being above all else. Books and articles regularly appear that tell her how to combine sex and parenting. It is simply a matter of logistics and having a soothing answer when Janie asks what that strange man is doing in mommy's bed. A whole new area called "divorce etiquette" is emerging to absolve the divorced mother of any guilt and at the same time supply her with an arsenal of answers for Janie's disturbing questions.

But the cultural emphasis on sex seldom helps the single mother put her life back together, and she often finds herself, after a year or so of the single life, in a worse place than she was before. She still must deal with grinding loneliness and, in addition, a diminished sense of self, for sleeping around does not heighten a woman's self-esteem.

Again, it is hard to be a mother in America today. The expectations established by the culture and by women themselves are demanding. Many mothers have responded to these expectations with vigor. They have taken up the gauntlet and have said, "I will do it *all.* I can manage marriage, parenting, sexual needs, and career demands quite well. Just watch me do it. It is simply a matter of time management and administrative skills. And guts."

Yet other mothers—and their number is growing—have nagging doubts and myriad frustrations. Many feel very much alone as they attempt to measure up to current cultural expectations. Mothers who work full-time wonder why they have so little time for their families and for themselves. Other women seem to manage. And housewives wonder why they don't feel better about themselves and their decision to stay home with their children.

My contacts with women and their children indicate that, no matter what the culture contends, we women cannot do it all. Numerous women are finding that they are trapped in schedules they can little control. Moreover, they sense a growing estrangement from their children and spouses.

What is wrong? Does the problem lie with the woman herself? Or are current cultural expectations unrealistic?

4

Working Mothers Have It All

> If women accept success to the same extent and in the same way that men do, the problems will be enormous. If women simply adopt the "number oneism" that dominates the workplace, the drive for achievement will probably lead them into the same narrowing and unpromising obsession that destroys men.
>
> S. M. Miller

By 1980 an estimated 52 percent of American women had joined the labor force.[1] According to 1979 U. S. Bureau of Labor Statistics, 59.1 percent of married women in the labor force had children ages 6–17 and 43.2 percent had children under the age of 6. Among divorced mothers in the labor force, 83.4 percent had children ages 6–17 and 68.9 percent had children 6 and under. Why have mothers gone to work in such record numbers? The reasons are varied.

A growing segment of the female population, the separated and divorced, work because they feel they have no other option. Only a minority of divorced fathers regularly pay child support, so the divorced mother either finds a job or becomes a name on the welfare rolls. And even when she works full-time, the divorced mother usually experiences a significant drop in her standard of living. Consequently, more divorced women than married women work.

Many women work to augment their husbands' modest salaries, which inflation has seriously eroded. According to statistics from the U. S. Department of Labor, in 1979 the median family income was $21,600 if the husband and wife worked and $16,600 if only the husband worked. In *The Two Paycheck Marriage,* author Caroline Bird said it another way: "Working wives lifted millions of families into middle-class life."

The salaries of working wives provide many of the extras of life, such as skiing lessons for children, family vacations, additional appliances, better-quality clothing. Said one young girl, "My brother and I will be able to go to summer camp because our mother is working." As they increase their families' goods and advantages, many women feel extremely gratified.

Other women, however, do not work strictly for economic reasons, but to flesh out an identity. Many simply cannot tolerate the lonely, empty hours that can plague the housewife. Said one mother, "I get moody when I don't work and am home alone. I am a much happier person when I am employed." Recently I spoke to a woman whose husband earns a high salary. This woman works as a secretary because she does not care for bridge or tennis and is bored at home.

An additional number of women work to satisfy personal ambition. The woman who finishes law school in her late thirties and lands a job with a prestigious Wall Street firm works to prove to herself and her family that she can do it—that she can excel and achieve some of her personal goals. She accepts the hour-and-a-half commute from home to office and the work reserved for rookies in any law firm because she has experienced the heady feeling that comes from achievement.

And women who are educated before they begin child-rearing feel an obligation to use their training in the marketplace. The fear that the brain power they fail to use may be lost forever becomes a powerful motivational force.

As women go off to work, a few quickly scale the heights in fields hitherto occupied chiefly by men, and some fortunates command excellent salaries. As these successful women make it up the corporate ladder, as they are offered partnerships in old and prestigious law firms, as they establish lucrative medical practices, they call down to their female counterparts and say, "Come on up. The air is wonderful up here." And using this comparative handful of women as role models and the unexamined ideas of the culture as chart and compass, other women join the labor force and attempt to scale similar heights.

WORKING MOTHERS HAVE A STRONGER SENSE OF IDENTITY

A powerful idea circulating in the culture today is that salary purchases a major slice of one's identity. A woman's worth (just as a man's) is now based on the money she earns. Since only in the marketplace do women get paid for services rendered, this means, in effect, that only working mothers, and not their stay-at-home counterparts, feel good about themselves and possess a strong sense of self.

Implicit in this idea is the assumption that the more a woman earns, the better she will feel about herself. The woman's goal thus becomes a position at the top of the corporate ladder. However, some women learn what men have learned in their scramble to the top: the ascent can be lonely and the losses experienced considerable. One occasionally reads in *Fortune* of a corporation president who literally lives in his office, except for those few hours on Sunday when he visits his children who live with his divorced wife. Workaholics, while they may succeed in business, often lose their families on the way up. Many successful men have discovered that work is only one aspect of life and that the joy of success palls when no one is there to share it.

This value system—basing one's worth and identity on what one earns—poses additional difficulties for the working mother. She may become a corporate executive, but she is still a wife and mother. As such, she has the difficult task of juggling the various aspects of her life and of feeling good about the kind of person she is in all areas of her life. Janet, who works for a Fortune 500 company, illustrates the dilemma of the working mother. Successful at work, Janet worries about her children and the long hours they are unsupervised after school and during summer vacations. "They watch too much television and seldom talk to me about their feelings. It's hard to be happy with my life when I'm so concerned about my children." Thus, a working mother is particularly vulnerable to unease if she feels her performance as a parent is lacking.

While the culture presses women to find their identities in work, seldom does the media portray the negative side of the world of work. Little is written about the long hours, the petty squabbles that often ensue, the sometimes boring routine, the unappreciative superiors, or the fact that few women are Harvard M.B.A.s earning thirty to fifty thousand dollars yearly.

Most women work on considerably lower rungs of the ladder, not as a Margaret Mead or a Barbara Walters, and their earnings are in the ten to fifteen thousand dollar range. This is fine if they do not expect to receive the acclaim of a Margaret Mead or the salary of the Harvard M.B.A. when they enter the marketplace. But if they base their identities on money earned, knowing that opportunities are limited, they are setting themselves up for disillusionment.

WORKING MOTHERS HAVE MORE FUN

Another prevailing idea is that women who work have more fun. Work, it seems, not only puts money in the pocket and introduces one to a new community of fellow workers, but it virtually insures happiness. Author Caroline Bird writes effusively about the rich life of the working mother and feels it is far superior to the poor housewife's lot. She notes that "working women live longer and feel better all along the way."

> Compared with homemakers, they are more apt to smoke, drink wine, eat out, travel abroad, join clubs, see films, read magazines, try new recipes, redecorate, cook gourmet meals, keep a dog or cat, follow the news, carry a credit card, insure their lives, keep up with the latest fashions, and go shopping for clothes and the house.[2]

In our consumer-oriented society, it is difficult to be poor or to have less than the lavish lifestyle written about in *Time* or *Newsweek*. Carl and Sherry are a one-paycheck family, and Carl earns less than twenty thousand yearly. Once when my husband and I were having dinner with them, Carl said, "I hate shopping at the malls. I see so much that I wish I had and I feel my clothes are outdated. Shopping titillates my greed and creates discontent."

If Carl's wife, mother of a small daughter, worked, then Carl and Sherry could purchase more goods. Would they then, in turn, have more fun? If one equates consumption with fun or happiness, then perhaps they would. If, on the other hand, one focuses on measures of happiness other than materialism, then one wonders if working wives (and their husbands) are indeed happier.

WORKING MOTHERS ARE SEXIER

Another tantalizing cultural idea is that working mothers are sexier than their stay-at-home counterparts. Jean Curtis, who wrote the book *Working Mothers*, definitely feels this is true. She mentions one woman who did not have orgasms until she went to work; then she learned that she was indeed an orgasmic creature, but not from sex with her husband. Rather, she discovered this personal truth when she began to have affairs. While Curtis is quick to note that less than 5 percent of the 200 women she interviewed had affairs, she does say that "many women report marital problems as a consequence of leaving home to 'go out into the world of men.' With or without affairs, many women feel their sex lives have changed."

Why is this so? Jean Curtis cites several reasons. First, working women begin to develop a separate identity. Their workaday world is unvisited by their families. Then, too, they find that just leaving the routine of home and family is pure excitement. They develop a new public image and are viewed differently by husbands, children, and friends. Moreover, working women experience the rebirth of long-forgotten goals, and this is a positive factor in their lives. All of these discoveries change their self-image and, in the process, their sex lives.[3]

Take the simple matter of wardrobe. When a woman is not working, it is hard to justify the expenditure of money to purchase an extensive wardrobe. More often than not, money is limited and the husband who works every day has a bigger clothes budget than his wife. The working mother, however, not only must have sufficient clothing for her work, but also has the money to spend. I have never met a woman who did not feel sexier when she had attractive clothes. *Any* woman will discover that she feels better about herself when she faces the day showered, groomed, and smartly dressed.

If the working mother has the time and the freedom to exploit her increased opportunities and her good feelings about herself, she may indeed lead a sexier life. But she is, after all, committed to her career for many of her waking hours. At work she is under pressure to produce and this, coupled with the stress of all her other roles, may limit sexual desire. Sexual feelings often grow in fallow, leisure hours. If studies were done on the sex lives of working mothers, one wonders what the results would show. From my informal sampling, I venture this: Working mothers have only so much time and energy, and they use most of it between nine and five. Thus, while working may produce a better self-image, it does not necessarily follow that a working mother will have either more, or better, sex.

Furthermore, Linda Wolfe, writing on love and work in *New York* magazine (February 16, 1981), says that the dual-career couple is severely stressed. "Instead of co-existing blissfully, many dual-career couples are wrestling continuously with professional rivalry; guilt about neglecting each other or their children, friends, and relatives; and performance anxiety both on the job and in the home."[4] As we all know, stress, guilt, and anxiety affect sexual feelings and performance.

WORKING MOTHERS ARE SUPERWOMEN

Another part of the working mother image is that she can do everything. An efficient administrator, a devoted parent, an alert and active sexual partner, the working mother leaves the stay-at-home mother in the dust. Long after the housewife has collapsed in exhaustion and trundled off to bed, the working mother is just getting her second wind. She is having her weekly "quality time" with her children while the washing machine hums in the background. After sharing dinner with her family and doing the dishes, our working mother is ready for an evening of Harvey's Bristol Creme and sex. If there is time left over, she will wash her nylons and iron a blouse.

This image obviously contains some truth. Working wives, as well as housewives, accomplish more when the work load increases. We have all experienced the lift that comes from the productive life, the feeling that we are operating at a higher level than we do when we have too many hours to structure and there is little to fill the time. The working mother has to be organized to get out of bed in the morning, and efficiency gives her an added lift.

A number of women have reported to me that their lives require the structure imposed by a job. Said one sales executive, "I had difficulty structuring all those hours. I found myself getting depressed when I had nothing in my life but my children. Working gets me going and I'm happier because of it."

There is, however, a flip side to this image which needs examination. Since I work at home as a writer and am able to set my own pace, I asked a woman who had returned to work six months earlier if the image of "super administrator" fit. Kathy agreed that she was now better organized and more efficient, but she felt the idea of supermother was a myth. "I do not have much leisure time with the children. Most of the time I am barking orders at them because now they have more work to do around the house and are not yet as productive as they need to be. My daughter, who is eleven, resents the fact that she has to care for her younger brother after school and begin preparation for supper. She and I have had some painful scenes. . . .

"Sex? Jim and I are often so tired after fulfilling all of our obligations that when we finally do get to bed at night we are content just to give each other a drowsy hug and kiss." Obviously, this couple will have to do what other busy couples are doing—they will need to move sex up the priority list and schedule time for it.

Time and energy. Working mothers find that time becomes a precious commodity when ten hours or more are lopped off daily for the business of work. Add the job to the task of running a house (even with husband and children helping out) and time with children, and many couples simply postpone their personal relationships until the weekend, sandwiching other activities into the hours that are left.

An article by Ann Marie Cunningham in *Savvy* magazine indicates that the lives of some of the country's successful women are barely worth living. Desiring to examine the lives of fifteen successful women, "aged 32–57—married and single, with and without children," *Savvy* asked these women to write "dispatches from the front." They were to keep a record of their daily lives from the moment the alarm rang until they went to bed. "*Savvy's* study meant to examine the quality of the lives of this vanguard group, women on the edge of time, who have achieved the female version of the American Dream."[5] The women were asked to log their thoughts and feelings as well as their activities.

What did the *Savvy* study reveal? The logs "give a general impression of constant activity, of virtual enslavement to schedule." Rising early in the morning (no one slept past 7:00 A.M.), these women moved through their days like "well oiled machines" and often worked until late at night. While Cunningham notes that the average male executive works a 60 hour week, one woman in the *Savvy* study who is a partner in a public relations firm worked 100 hours out of the 122 logged.

Husbands and sex got scant attention in the logs of these successful women. One failed to mention her husband until the third page of her log, and only "two women, both married, reported sex (with their husbands, once each)." Either fatigue cancelled out their sexual urges, says Cunningham, or the women were "ignoring a source of replenishment and comfort."

One of the conclusions of the *Savvy* article is that the women studied "lead rather austere lives."

> The logs suggest that while opportunities for women have burgeoned, quality of lives has declined. To do what we love best, we have sacrificed many simple pleasures, including sleep, privacy, friends, nest-building, pets, home-cooked food, and in some cases, children. No log keeper had time simply to sit and think—which sometimes was the very thing she was paid to do. Some had no time to spend their money in enjoyable ways. Others were obliged to pay heavily for housekeepers, surrogate wives and a plethora of other time-saving services. "Home" is stripped down to a place "that works"; "wardrobe" to "clothes that function."[6]

With little or no time for pleasure, these successful mothers also had minimal time for their children. Jane E. Brody, science writer for *The New York Times,* whose day included tennis and swimming as well as time at the office, a speech at the "Y", and work on the galleys of her nutrition book, finally arrived home at 10:30 P.M. for supper and a conversation with her boys and her husband.

Another mother, Mary Didie, who works as a physician earning more than $35,000 per year, has three children under the age of five. Described as "wrung out" from the various roles that take her away from home and children from 9:00 A.M. to 7:00 P.M. daily, Mary Didie wondered in her log if she were spending enough time with her young children.

And I wonder too. For years I have struggled with the cultural idea that "it is quality and not quantity time that counts." Is this motto just a sop for parental guilt? Who has ever defined this magical "quality time" when psychic wounds are healed and children derive enough good stuff to go on living and growing? Is it ten minutes a day or twenty minutes a week? Is it time alone with each child or is it a group activity? Is it watching television silently while bodies merely occupy the same general space?

I read of one government official who was away from home for long hours each day. This woman has a large family and mentioned that her "quality time" with one particular daughter occurred during the few minutes when she fixed the girl's hair. While I do not doubt that this daily ritual could be imbued with meaning or that the girl could often postpone her needs until the appointed hour, is it possible that real intimacy can occur when the daughter knows that her mother has only ten or fifteen minutes at the most to give her? Granted, if the child's heart were breaking, her mother would schedule more time later. But what about meeting the child's need at the moment of need? Working mothers lack that flexibility.

We recognize that good marriages require time, effort, and energy. Is it any different with good parenting? Don't our children need "quantity time" with us so that they can, when necessary, speak from their hearts? Or are they better able than we to postpone emotional needs until there's a break in our schedule and it is convenient for us to communicate with them?

I often envision this scenario: I as a busy, productive person come to my younger daughter, Kristen, and say, "I cannot talk to you today, dear, but tomorrow at precisely eight o'clock we will have our 'quality time.' Then in the ten minutes allotted you can tell me all your hurts, I will answer all your questions about life, and we will be close."

I have never done this nor could I. My children, I believe, need daily access to me during part of their at-home, waking hours. Just yesterday Kristen came home from school and motioned for me to follow her into her room. She started to weep. Jennie, the girl Kristen wants as her best friend, told the teacher that Susie was her best friend. Kristen had suspected that this was so but had wished to be the most important friend in Jennie's life.

I held my child close as she sobbed and tried to share some of my mother wisdom. I mentioned that most of us have only a few best friends as we travel through life, and time spent in their company yields moments of grace. We cannot *try* to become someone's best friend; when we are fortunate enough to find that close friend, we come together because of chemistry and mutual interests.

Kristen listened and in a few moments was busy again with her life. Later that evening she said, "It doesn't hurt as much any more that Jennie doesn't want me to be her best friend," and she smiled.

What does a child do with emotional needs or wounds from the day when he comes home to an empty house and mother is working? Jean Curtis in *Working Mothers* notes: "The children of working mothers often have to wait until the end of the day for maternal solace."[7] This is all well and good if the child will talk at the end of the day and if the parent has enough energy and presence of mind to listen. Sometimes, however, tired parents are too embroiled in their own problems to listen attentively. Or children may be unwilling to shift the talking time from after school to late evening. Instead, they learn to internalize any hurt.

Jean Curtis mentions one mother whose child would not make the shift. Before Pat went to work, her daughter Sally talked to her in the late afternoon when Pat prepared supper. Although the daughter still had the opportunity to talk to her working mother after the evening meal, she chose not to do so. Said the mother, "If you ask me what I had to give up when I went back to work, I'd say it was that—my talks with Sally. She's my only daughter and, you know, that's a lot to give up."[8]

Granted, it is possible to schedule time alone with

each child and with one's husband. Sally Olds, who wrote *The Mother Who Works Outside the Home,* says that working mothers have to schedule time with their children wisely since

> you have less time than your stay-at-home counterpart to be with your children, less time to express your love for them, less time to find out what's on their minds, less time to just have fun together. So you need to plan your time more, to make the most of every minute.[9]

Even ten minutes alone with each child daily is a powerful thing, according to Dr. Richard Gardner, author of *The Boys and Girls Book About Divorce.* Some mothers achieve this with ease; but it is hard for others to do this consistently, particularly if they are continuously pressed. It is hard for us humans to do anything consistently, pressed or not. And when steady pressure is mixed with too little time, is it likely that we will maintain closeness with each member of our family?

WORKING MOTHERS HAVE HAPPIER, MORE INDEPENDENT CHILDREN

Another idea in vogue is that once children reach the age of eight or nine, they are quite able to be alone for certain portions of the day or night. In fact, if we do not leave them alone, we thwart their growth toward independence. Since independence is one of *the* American virtues, we look for those life experiences that will nurture this trait. What better way to develop this spirit of independence than to have children return to an empty house after school? Alone, they can learn to care for younger siblings, do their homework, start supper, discipline themselves enough to pick up the house—the list goes on and on. And it does seem that children of working mothers develop independence.

An article entitled "Four Bright Children Speak Out on Having *Both* Parents Work" supports this idea. Perry, age eleven, says, "It's hard to say if I'd want my mother to be home all the time. It's basically up to her. I don't mind because I like to be more independent." And Bill, also eleven, who comments that his parents are often away, offers this: "They could go out more and I wouldn't mind it. I seem to like privacy a lot, go 'round to the park, hang out a bit. I like it."

But Jed, who is twelve, has this bit of child wisdom to share. When a friend of his said he would like to have both parents work so that he could become more independent, Jed countered, "I think that's silly because when you're a kid, that's your chance to have someone to depend on. Why not use that time to have somebody to depend on, and then when you grow older you can learn to depend on yourself?"[10]

While many working mothers value independence as a worthy trait, some worry about their children's physical safety. Some attempt to offer supervision via written instructions or over the phone. As they sit in their offices watching the clock, knowing that their children are due home, these working mothers often call to check in. This is their attempt to communicate love and interest to their children and in the process allay any fears or concerns they might have about leaving their children alone after school.

Other mothers encourage their children to stay in a locked house or close to home because they feel their children are safer this way. Safety, after all, comes from knowledge that doors can be locked and the stay-at-home mother next door can be called in case of emergencies. How many working mothers and their children have an unspoken reliance on the neighbor who chooses to stay home with her children?

And what about those older children who have less need of safety and greater need to test out life experiences, namely sex, drugs, and alcohol? Do these children who walk around in adult bodies need any daily supervision? It is naïve to believe that older children will not use the empty house for afternoon sexual encounters or experiments with drugs or alcohol. Teen-agers tell me that this is a common experience.

When I was a child, I accompanied several other girls and boys to a classmate's empty house for a few hours of unsupervised fun. Although we were too young to do more than play spin the bottle, I remember the excitement in the air, the knowledge that no adult was present or likely to appear. This was a heady and somewhat frightening experience.

Some parents apparently are not alarmed to think that their young might experiment with drugs or sex or alcohol within the environs of home. Perhaps they feel that this is part of growing up in America today. Freedom to experiment with various aspects of life is, after all, part of American adolescence. One mother who attended a seminar on drugs later told me that the speaker said that parents should just assume that their children would experiment with marijuana. This mother had already come to terms with this as a given for her young children.

However, one father who overheard her account of the seminar became irate. "What right has any so-called authority to tell me to assume my child will use marijuana. I plan to assume otherwise."

Whatever a parent's attitudes toward teen-ager's experiments with life, the fact remains that unsupervised adolescents often get into trouble. I interviewed one policeman in an affluent lake community who said that most of the burglaries in the neighborhood occurred in the afternoon—while parents worked. He felt that adolescents need greater parental supervision and restraint so that they will not be such a burden on the police force and the community.

While the culture applauds the mother who leaves home for the marketplace, what do her children think of her? Are all her children so overcome with pride in her accomplishments that they never miss her presence late in the day or never wish she were physically present to act as teacher or companion?

No child that I interviewed enjoyed coming home to an empty house or remaining home alone when he was sick. All the children indicated that at such times they longed for mother-presence and mother-solace. This holds true for older children as well as younger. The fact that a child of fourteen may look like an adult does not diminish his desire for a caring adult at certain times in life.

As one reads the current articles and books on working mothers, one fact becomes increasingly clear: the literature focuses almost exclusively on mother and her needs. It is *her* fulfillment, *her* life we find so absorbing. If mother will only find her career, make the appropriate sacrifices, and earn a lot of money, then all will be well.

But what about mother's children who have to fit into *her* life in some capacity? What about *the child's need* to have at least one parent emotionally and physically present a good deal of the time? As one working mother said recently, "My husband and I are seldom home. We use this house as a place to sleep, change clothes, and eat a few hurried meals." She said nothing about her children who are home alone for many hours after school and during the evening.

To be intellectually honest, we must consider the effect of the dual-career marriage on children if it means they grow up virtually alone. We must ask ourselves if we are having a negative impact upon our children in immeasurable ways that will only become evident with the passage of time.

And while the media presses women to advance in

their careers and "make it" in a male-dominated society, it is well to consider one marriage and divorce counselor's comment:

> The higher the position the woman has achieved and the more responsibility she has assumed, the greater the strain upon her and the more time she will have to spend away from her children.[11]

To work or not to work? It's no easy decision.

---

[1]*U. S. News and World Report* (December 8, 1980), p. 51.
[2]Caroline Bird, *The Two Paycheck Family* (New York: Rawson, Wade, Publishers, Inc., 1979), p. 38.
[3]Jean Curtis, *Working Mothers* (New York: Doubleday and Co., Inc., 1976), pp. 148–51.
[4]Linda Wolfe, "Love and Work: How to Succeed," *New York Magazine* (February 16, 1981), p. 29.
[5]Ann Marie Cunningham, "The Time Pressured Life," *Savvy* (December, 1980), pp. 38–52.
[6]Ibid., p. 50.
[7]Curtis, *Working Mothers*, p. 69.
[8]Ibid., p. 53.
[9]Sally Olds, *The Mother Who Works Outside the Home* (Child Study Press, 1975), p. 22.
[10]*New Woman* (April, 1979).
[11]Dr. F. Philip Rice, *A Working Mother's Guide to Child Development* (Englewood Cliffs, New Jersey: Prentice-Hall, Inc., 1979), p. 77.

5

The Empty Housewife

> No matter how much we reassure her, the homemaker knows she is only a housewife. Whatever we say, the proof is clear: She receives no pay for what she does.
>
> Jessie Bernard

WHILE THE CULTURE applauds the full-time working mother, it denigrates the woman who chooses to stay home, without pay, to pursue the art of housewifery and to rear her children. The very desire to rear one's young is viewed as a modern evil. Hear Louise J. Kaplan, director of Child Clinical Services and associate professor of psychology at the City University of New York:

> Certainly nowhere is the disparagement of the biological more evident than in our current view of motherhood. Motherhood has come into conflict with our post-industrial mentality, a mentality that locates a person's most significant activity outside the home and therefore questions the possibility of self-realization through motherhood. The self-absorbing solitude of mother and infant is interpreted as a lamentable turning away from activity that is considered more socially productive.[1]

Because of this disparagement of motherhood, many women today have postponed childbearing. As she approaches her mid-thirties, however, the woman who has given all to career realizes that her years of childbearing are running out. Her gynecologist issues dire warnings about having that first child after thirty-five. At this point in her life, the career woman must either say yes to motherhood or decide to remain childless.

Even if she decides to have a child, our career woman may discover that this option is foreclosed to her. In an article entitled "Barren Couples," Miriam D. Mazor writes that "there has been an increase in the number of people in the United States who find they are unable to conceive children." Since men and women are most fertile in their mid-twenties, when they postpone marriage and childbearing until their thirties or forties, they often discover that biology is working against them. According to Mazor, "approximately one out of every six married couples of childbearing age, or 3.5 million couples, are believed to have some difficulty conceiving or carrying a pregnancy to term."[2]

But what about those who do conceive? Even the most avid feminists sometimes wax eloquent in print about the ecstasy of carrying that first baby. And when the child is born, some feminists find that biology has turned the tables on them. Once stridently vocal about the evils of staying home with children, they now feel the strange stirrings of something that ties them to their young. They begin to experience the struggles that other mothers have had before them. They feel responsible for, and want to be with, their babies. Some feminists articulate this inner struggle in articles heavy with apology. They seem to feel that in wishing to be with their babies they have betrayed their whole sex.

For feminists and traditionalists alike, this struggle is real indeed. Does our successful career-woman-turned-mother, or any other mother for that matter, stay at home and don a negative cultural image as she raises her child, or does she find someone else to care for her child so that she can pick up the threads of her "real" life?

> Legions of women who wish to have children and devote themselves for a time to the care of their children are shamed into believing that such a wish amounts to a capitulation to sexist or antiquated social values intended to exile them to a doll's house. In the rush "to return to normal," to "get on with the business of real life" and compete in the race for career and social advancement, the modern mother is deprived of her rightful experience of mothering.[3]

Dr. Kaplan points out that a woman's need to respond to her baby "leisurely and sensitively" has been subverted by cultural pressures. Yet she believes it is this "elemental dialogue between mother and infant" that insures the continuance of our humanity.

But various factors make it hard to choose to stay home with one's children. Writing in *McCalls,* Ellen Goodman states, "Until the 1970's it was most often the employed mother who felt the harsh judgment of society: She was the one criticized and put down by both men and women, especially by the mothers at home." Now, however, cultural ideals and attitudes have changed. No longer does the stay-at-home mother win any of society's approbation for her stance. Goodman continues: "As working mothers receive the praise of society, the women at home have begun to feel keenly a loss of status and with it, a loss of self-esteem."[4]

In her interviews with housewives, Goodman found them "defensive and angry." Though they had chosen to stay home because they felt their children needed them, they were troubled. They realized that not only did they stand against their culture, but they often lacked the full support of their husbands in the process.

At a recent party I watched a husband press his wife to go to work. Although he earns a generous salary as a corporate lawyer, this man stated that he wanted his wife to work so that her life would be more fulfilling. He felt they had little to discuss on long winter evenings. Their children were twelve and under, but this husband voiced no need for his wife to be home after school. On the contrary, he felt that all she did after school was chauffeur the kids around anyway.

The wife reacted with deep hostility to her husband's comments as she nervously tried to defend her decision to stay home. She stated that she was not trained for a profession and did not wish to work in a menial capacity just to be able to say that she was employed. It was obvious that this was an old and painful argument.

This husband's feelings were echoed by a friend of ours in a recent Christmas letter in which he wrote that while he is involved in a busy and thriving business, his wife spends many hours chauffeuring the kids around—"the sad lot of the suburban housewife."

This mentality erodes a housewife's belief that her work has merit. If the culture does not value her role or, worse yet, if her husband feels she is wasting her time, she will either capitulate and go out to work or retrench in anger and defensiveness.

Whether a woman stays home to mother her young children or simply because she loves her home and has no desire to go to work, she often finds herself in the position of justifying her choice to her friends, her husband, even herself. Her lot is painful in the extreme as she contends with both cultural accusations and her own inner questioning.

HIDING OUT IN SUBURBIA

One of the cultural accusations facing the mother who stays home is that she is afraid to test herself in the marketplace and is hiding out in suburbia. Feeling that she could not find a good job or earn a reasonable salary, our stereotypical housewife fills up her hours with trivia or continues having children so that she can avoid facing the market value of her skills. If the housewife is uneducated and unskilled, then her contemporaries may offer her pity; but if she is educated, no quarter is given.

Doesn't the educated housewife know that Betty Friedan opened her prison doors with the publication of *The Feminine Mystique* in the sixties? With Friedan sounding the clarion call, educated housewives in droves have successfully traded aprons and vacuums for suits and attache cases. Any educated mother who chooses to stay home faces the burden of wondering if it is true that she will fall hopelessly behind in the race for the worthwhile life. If she waits, she may not find a decent job when her children no longer need her. This concern can produce deep anxiety.

It is true that some women remain at home because they fear testing themselves in the marketplace. And rightly so. If one has been a housewife for twenty years and has no college education, it is alarming to envision a new life as an employed person. It is natural to wonder if one can get a good job and compete with younger, better-educated women. Also, one has to deal with the problem of inertia and the fact that it is easier to stay in a known rut than to venture into the unknown. Nor is transition from home to marketplace made any easier by the fact that the housewife starts from a weak position—from the low status she has in society.

Many older women find, however, that when they brush up on skills or enroll at the local university, they possess marketable attributes: their intelligence, experience, and determination to succeed. Some of my best university students were women in their early fifties who happily discovered that those years at home did not rot their brains and that they were just as intelligent as much younger women. Older, they brought to their classes a richer perspective on life. Since they were finished with child-rearing, these students were able to devote their full energies to education and any subsequent career.

BEING A HOUSEWIFE MAKES A WOMAN SICK

Another powerful idea circulating in the culture is that the woman who stays home is a candidate for an asylum. One reads in Jessie Bernard's *The Future Of Marriage* that "being a housewife makes women sick."[5] Bernard supports her inflammatory statement with studies showing that the mental health of the housewife is poorer than the mental health of the working woman. Bernard blames this deterioration on the fact that the housewife is home alone, isolated except for the company of her children.[6]

Maggie Scarf, author of *Unfinished Business,* disagrees. She notes that a recent investigation conducted by the Yale Depression Unit compared a matching sample of women who worked with traditional housewives. Their finding? "Housewives and working wives were *equally* prone to depression." To be female, says Scarf, is simply to be more vulnerable than males to depression.[7] Interestingly, the husbands of working wives were *more* prone to depression than were husbands of housewives.

Admittedly, the housewife has to work hard to avoid being isolated. Mothers often go to great lengths to organize play groups for their young children, not only so that the children will have contacts, but so the mothers will also. Other women join numerous organizations, hoping to find friendships. Even so, the housewife usually has far more solitude than the working mother.

While some women wilt in aloneness, others thrive on solitude and use solitary time as an opportunity to paint or read or write or garden or do handwork or simply reflect. It is not inevitable that the mother at home succumb to depression. In a sense, we only confront our real selves when we are alone. And in our aloneness, we can develop a fair share of the discipline or inner strength needed to create meaningful lives.

ANY WOMAN WHO STAYS HOME IS WASTING HER LIFE

Finally, we come to the most debilitating accusation of all: The woman who chooses to stay home to rear her children is wasting her life. Not only will her children function better in her absence, but she is, in the final analysis, an unnecessary appendage to her husband's life. All the services she renders, with the possible exception of the sexual, can be purchased from a domestic or a gardener or a day-care center. In short, mother would do better to trade in her unsalaried job as housewife and caretaker and join her contemporaries in the marketplace.

This accusation is particularly threatening because sooner or later, housewives ask themselves: *Am I wasting my life? Will time wash away all that I am doing so that when I die there will be nothing left to show that I have lived?* Of course, it is not only the housewife who awakens in the middle of the night in a state of cold panic to confront this existential question. To be human is to ask if one's life has any ultimate meaning.

Inundated with cultural propaganda, the housewife finds it easier to feel that she is wasting her life than does the working mother. The housewife has no paycheck to signify her market value, no objects that she has purchased with her salary, no career advancement to brag about at her husband's yearly Christmas party. She works with intangibles like her children's view of the world and the atmosphere she creates in her home.

Some women have enough inner strength and self-esteem to reject the cultural assessment of their worth. I met one such woman in a church one Tuesday morning when I went to observe one of the regular sessions designed to provide support for the women of this particular church which strongly values the traditional roles of wife and mother.

When I asked this attractive woman in her late twenties about the way she viewed herself and her life, she said without apology, "I stay home rearing my children because I believe I am raising America's future generation. Is anything more valuable than this?" With that she smiled and guided two small children out of the room. As she left, I could not help admiring her strongmindedness and her belief that what she was doing with her life had enormous value.

The time does come for most women, however, when something inside cries out, "There must be more to life than this." When this moment of truth comes, a woman realizes that she cannot live for her husband and children. If she has examined the career issue closely, she realizes that she cannot live for a job. If she is wise, she also knows she cannot live for herself.

Even as she enumerates the things she cannot live for, a woman asks what is big enough, deep enough, absorbing enough to demand her total self? The answer, as we shall see in the latter part of the book, is found in confronting the spiritual dimension of her life.

---

[1]Louise J. Kaplan, *Oneness and Separateness: From Infant to Individual* (New York: Simon and Schuster, 1978), p. 26.
[2]Miriam D. Mazor, "Barren Couples," *Psychology Today* (May, 1979), p. 101.
[3]Kaplan, *Oneness*, p. 26.
[4]Ellen Goodman, "The Changing World of the Full-Time Housewife," *McCalls* (February, 1979), p. 85.
[5]Jessie Bernard, *The Future of Marriage* (New York: World Publishing Co., 1972), p. 48.
[6]Ibid., pp. 46–47.
[7]Maggie Scarf, *Unfinished Business: Pressure Points in the Lives of Women* (New York: Doubleday and Co., 1980), p. 529.

6

The Swinging Cosmo Mother

> Many of my clients have been badly hurt by the pain of multiple separations from many different partners. That, to me, is the most negative aspect of the sexual revolution.
>
> Dr. Helen Colton

WHETHER SHE IS divorced, widowed, or has never married, the single mother has a demanding life. She confronts the dual tasks of working and rearing her children without significant help. As she struggles to do both, often alone and lonely, she soon discovers that society views her as a super-sexual being and that most married women see her as a predator.

Rightfully, many single mothers chafe at this image. When I taught classes on separation and divorce at the University of North Carolina in Asheville, I met single women who were angry that most of their married female friends viewed them with suspicion.

As with any stereotype, this one contains a measure of truth. Single women, particularly those coming out of a bad marriage, are vulnerable, and the divorced, and the widowed as well, generally are not known for their sexual abstinence. In a study entitled "Postmarital Coitus Among Widows and Divorcees," Paul Gebhard states that of those studied, 82 percent of the divorced and 43 percent of the widowed experienced postmarital coitus early in their life alone.[1] Among the divorced, three-fourths began having sexual encounters within the first year alone as compared with one half of the widowed.[2]

Apparently, widows, because of their greater financial stability, the quality of their marital relationship, and the trauma of grief, avoid or postpone the advent of sexual encounters. Divorced women, on the other hand, have no fond memories of an idealized spouse to discourage the pursuit of sexual relationships.

Gebhard notes that "many women begin to have extramarital relationships during the final stages of marriage and continue sexual relationships with lovers through the breakup of the marriage and after the divorce." For the majority of the divorced, this pattern of frequent and open sexuality continues throughout the years alone, even when they have custody of their children.

Mel Krantzler, who wrote the best-selling *Creative Divorce*, has published its sequel, *Learning To Love Again*. In this book he holds himself up as a model for the single population, implying that what worked for him will work for others.

In this second book, Krantzler writes mainly about his relationship with Pat, the woman he lived with for nearly a year and later married. Pat has an adolescent daughter who apparently joined her mother in this living-together arrangement. No mention is made about any possible negative effects of this arrangement on the girl. Nor does Krantzler postulate just how the girl would have been affected if his relationship with her mother had ended before marriage. He writes primarily about sexual pleasure for a sexually oriented readership and even believes the new trend toward living together is "moral."

Some single mothers have written about their sexual relationships with the idea that their children will ultimately profit from mother's openness. One book, *Sex and the Single Parent* by Jane Adams, speaks graphically of the author's sexual experiences and of her occasional unease about her children, who waited just outside the bedroom door.

While Jane Adams, divorced mother, sees nothing wrong with her casual sexual encounters, she feels conflict about just how her children will view them. On the one hand, she argues that if she brings a man home to bed, it's okay if he stays all night and meets her children the next day. But she's not comfortable with her open minded stance. When her young daughter asked if she would bring someone home from a party to sleep over, Adams writes: "I realize it is too late for that innocence, and I am sad. So I do not invite him to spend the night and he leaves before sunup. And I wonder why I preserve the rituals when their meaning is long since forgotten."[3]

Obviously, current sexual mores are antithetical to the sexual ethic espoused in the Bible, namely that intercourse should occur only within marriage. But this fact in no way exempts mothers who are Christian and single from the pressures of a sexually oriented society. During the past ten years I have talked to many single Christian mothers struggling with their sexual needs. Most were sexually active. "Why not have sex?" they asked me. "Everybody else is." Because of their faith, they were not comfortable with their lifestyle. Yet they, just as non-Christians, had been bombarded by sexual myths.

HER AFFAIRS WON'T HARM HER CHILDREN

One of the prevailing cultural ideas is that children are not adversely affected by a parent's sexual experiences. This is so generally accepted that few custodial parents even go outside their homes for their sexual encounters. They end up in bed just down the hall from sleeping children to reenact, with minor differences, the scene from *Kramer vs. Kramer* where Billy stumbles out of bed only to confront his father's naked girl friend, also on her way to the bathroom. The titters in the theater where I saw this movie indicated that many of the viewers thought this little more than an embarrassing moment for father.

Magazine articles even provide something called "divorce etiquette" to deal with just this situation. Sadly, the articles fail to address Johnny's feelings and the possibility that his parent's open sexuality will have any lasting effect on his view of himself, sex, or the parent involved.

During my days as an editorial consultant I met enough boys and girls under twelve who were living with sexually active divorced mothers to question this popular wisdom. One mother, who later married her live-in lover, spoke of her son's marked deterioration during the period she and her lover experimented with open sexuality. Another woman who had a series of live-in lovers has a son who felt he had to steal in order to tell the world that his emotional needs were unmet. Yet another divorced mother told me of the difficulties she was having disciplining her children because she felt guilty about her sexual experiences. And recently a friend recounted the inner dilemma she is having because she, who is sexually active, does not want her teen-agers to follow in her footsteps. She is caught in the throes of her own hypocrisy.

What about the older child, the adolescent girl who is experiencing the emergence of her own sexual feelings? How does she respond to her single mother's sexuality? Fran, a mother I met several years ago, mentioned that her daughter became angry and hurt when Fran started to have lovers. In time the girl became sexually active herself. But Fran failed to note any connection between her behavior and her daughter's or to assume responsibility for her child's behavior.

The report "11 Million Teenagers," a publication of the Guttmacher Institute, a division of Planned Parenthood, states that of the twenty-one million young people in the U. S. between the ages of fifteen and nineteen, more than half, or some eleven million, have had sexual intercourse.

The report states that this increased sexual activity leads to increased illegitimate births. "Close to thirteen million of the 60 million women who became mothers in 1975 became parents before they became adults." Early childbearing is increasing everywhere, is now emerging as a serious problem in many countries, and has reached alarming levels in others. The report continues: "Adolescent pregnancy is a serious threat to the life and health of a young woman . . . whether the birth occurs in or out of a marriage."

Increased abortion is another direct result of increased adolescent sexual activity. The Guttmacher report indicates that "one-third of all abortions are obtained by teenagers," and since 1973 the rate of teen abortion has risen 60 percent.

Many of the teen-agers who seek abortions do not use contraception. Even with sex education in the public schools and the proliferation of Planned Parenthood Centers, some girls are woefully ignorant about contraception, while others do not wish to appear prepared for a sexual encounter. In *The Ambivalence of Abortion,* Linda Bird Francke interviewed several teen-age girls who had had two abortions before reaching the age of twenty. Many were nonchalant in their attitudes and viewed abortion as merely no-fail contraception. According to Francke, abortion clinic personnel become discouraged by teen-agers and older women who return for two or three abortions. Too often abortion clinics act as a kind of service station for sexually active but irresponsible females.[4]

The Guttmacher report, after viewing the situation of unwed mothers with alarm, draws some interesting conclusions. Reflecting present cultural values, it advocates realistic sex education, increased pregnancy counseling services, equal availability and accessibility of legal abortion in all parts of the nation, and health-care programs for mother and child, among other things. Nowhere does the report advocate abstinence for teen-agers who are too young to become parents, nor does it note any connection between open adult sexuality and the rise of adolescent sexual activity.

Does it take any great stretch of the imagination to believe that the little boy who imitates his father's walk will grow up to adopt, in large measure, his father's sexual values? Or is it unrealistic to assume that the fourteen-year-old girl will take her sexual cues from her divorced mother's behavior?

One twice-divorced mother who attended a seminar on separation and divorce that my husband and I gave told me that she had numerous open sexual flings after her first divorce, when her daughter was eleven. Later when the girl became sexually active and experienced painful relationships, the mother tried to advocate abstinence because she saw how her child was being hurt. The daughter, in anger, pointed out that she was merely modeling her behavior after her mother's. Her mother was effectively silenced.

One seldom discussed situation facing the single mother is the possibility that the lover, particularly if he moves into the household, may decide that he wants to sleep with the daughter as well as with the mother. Or perhaps the lover will bring an adolescent boy into the new arrangement and the son will have designs on the young girl.

Unlikely? Not so. Carol and her husband, Erik, are houseparents in a state-financed home for runaways called Cope House in Brevard, North Carolina. They have stated that many of the runaway girls who end up with them are fleeing the sexual advances of the mother's lover or lover's son. One girl said that when her mother's lover moved in he brought his son who assumed that he would sleep with the young girl. The girl chose to run away instead. Both Carol and Erik agree that the girls who come to them are deeply concerned about sexual morality—their mothers' in particular—and run away to escape untenable situations at home.

SLEEPING AROUND HEIGHTENS SELF-ESTEEM

Another explicit cultural message is that casual sex increases a woman's good feelings about herself. Numerous divorced women (and men, for that matter) indicate that they emerge from bad marriages so bruised and insecure about their sexuality that initial sexual encounters soothe the wounded ego and produce a temporary high. Said one mother, "When my former husband finished his number on me, I felt like worn-out merchandise. It was wonderful to discover with Stan, the first man I slept with, that I was okay sexually." Her experience is far from unique.

It is important to distinguish between the short-term effects of sleeping around and the long-term. The long-term effect of casual sex leaves many women feeling empty inside. In "The New Chastity," Paul Solomon writes of women who chose to be celibate for varying periods of time because they have been hurt by the experience of casual sex. They have found that "indiscriminate intercourse, sleeping with someone just because one feels one ought to be doing it, is ridiculous, even harmful. For them, the urgent, repetitive promiscuity of the past ten years has produced little but anxiety." Solomon quotes these women as saying:

> People are tired of *pain*. How many times have you heard somebody complain that every time she gets into a sexual relationship, she gets hurt? Sure we love sex, and won't ever stop loving it, but I think we're all fed up with the ego games that seem to go along with it. It's better to wait around chastely until you're truly swept away by love.
>
> This new chastity is more challenging, because the pressure from the culture is very strong *not* to be chaste. Most women feel about as satisfied after casual, perfunctory sex as they do after a sneeze.[5]

So casual sex hurts. One has only to read Shere Hite's book *The Hite Report*, a compilation of the results of a questionnaire filled out by 3,000 women, to discover that many women who have had numerous sexual partners feel exploited by men. Said one, "My greatest displeasure is to wake up the next morning with a man who had changed since we'd had sex—he wouldn't talk to me or react to anything the next day." In Hite's book numerous women speak of feeling used by men who were able to divorce sex from feeling. They felt they were little more than receptacles for the male organ.

Sadly, some women felt they had changed for the worse after years of painful sexual encounters.

> I started out when I was very young, open, natural, warm, spontaneous, uninhibited, and in ten years I've become bitter, cold, cynical, angry, resentful, hateful, frightened, and suspicious. I don't like it but that's where I've ended up. I suppose I hate men except the man who I live with. I think if we ever split I would be alone. I think I'm pretty dried up and old for twenty-one but maybe I'll die young.[6]

One of the questions I asked myself during my five years as a separated and divorced mother was what I would become if I slept with every man who entered my life. What kind of person would I become? I believed that I would get away with nothing and that I would accrue those "invisible marks on the soul." While my face might not reflect my life, something inside would change forever. And I did not believe that the change would be for the better.

Besides, how would I actually *feel* the morning after? Would I feel guilty, or, as the media says, womanly? And how would I respond to those two beautiful daughters gazing up at me with open, trusting faces? They would someday grow up and become teen-agers, and I knew I could never ask them to be chaste if I were not.

It was not easy to keep men out of my bed. My husband left our marriage for someone else, and the wounds caused by his rejection were deep. Like most who exit from a failing marriage, I hurt inside. And during that vulnerable first year alone I came close to having an affair with a married man. Only my relationship with Christ and the counseling of a good friend kept me from a sexual involvement.

From this experience, I knew that I had to find some antidote for my loneliness, and my need drove me to a Christian community where I was loved, affirmed, and substantially healed. When I returned to America, with the help of the Holy Spirit I was able to stand against cultural pressures.

The culture screamed sex and indicated that something was wrong if I was not hopping into bed with any available man. But God kept bringing women into my life who were having affairs, and I saw much pain and confusion in their lives and the lives of their children. I knew I didn't want that turmoil and guilt. Additionally, God sent strong, supportive Christians who openly encouraged me to live by the biblical sexual ethic. One, my dear friend Penny, was always there with a cup of tea, laughter, and encouragement when I needed her.

I learned a marvelous truth during my five years as a single parent: It is possible to come to terms with one's self as a warm, loving woman without hopping into bed with the available men.

When a man did enter my life whom I grew to love, I discovered other, unpublished rewards of attempting to follow the Christian sexual ethic. Don liked my values and admired the kind of woman I was. And he who had become a committed Christian wanted to remarry a woman with like commitment.

After our marriage I learned that nothing is lost in terms of sexual feeling during periods of celibacy. If anything, sexual feelings become more intense. When those wounds caused by rejection are largely healed and we have come to terms with ourselves as women, when we are not plagued by feelings of guilt, then the sexual aspect of marriage or remarriage can be wonderful—some days, glorious.

But what if we fail to live up to the rigorous standards God sets for His sons and daughters in the sexual area? And we all fail in some measure. Then we must ask for His forgiveness, pick ourselves up and go on. He is merciful and understands our frailties. We do need to be careful, though, and not equate forgiveness with condonation. God does not condone sin in any area, and His forgiveness does not eradicate the consequences of our sin. He sometimes allows us to feel the full weight of sorrow for wrongdoing. Said a friend about the sexual relationships she engaged in after she had become a Christian: "I felt an increasing sorrow about my past. I knew God had forgiven me, but it took longer for me to forgive myself. And the more I matured in my Christianity, the more clearly I realized just what I had done."

My friend is now liberated from both her sorrow and guilt, and she uses her past experience to warn other women to withstand the cultural pressures of the sexual revolution.

Having spent yesterday with a separated mother who is sexually involved with the wrong man and knows it, I realize anew just how difficult it is for the single mother to gut it out alone. Caught in the throes of loneliness and incredible psychic pain, few will stop to evaluate the consequences of a certain lifestyle. Understandably, most reach out to *any* help that's offered. And for the newly separated mother, help most often comes in the form of a man.

Thus begin those sexual relationships that never bring that promised joy.

---

[1]Paul Gebhard, "Postmarital Coitus Among Widows and Divorcees," *Divorce and After,* ed. Paul Bohannan (New York: Doubleday and Co., 1970), p. 93.
[2]Ibid., p. 97.
[3]Jane Adams, *Sex and the Single Parent* (New York: Coward, McCann and Geoghegan, Inc., 1978), p. 290.
[4]Linda Bird Francke, *The Ambivalence of Abortion* (New York: Random House, 1978), pp. 39–40.
[5]Paul Solomon, "The New Chastity," *Cosmopolitan* (January, 1979), pp. 148–49.
[6]Shere Hite, *The Hite Report* (New York: Dell, 1976), p. 469.

7

The Payoff

> Today some Americans worry that in the last decade or so the U. S. has . . . developed a distaste for children that sometimes seems almost to approach fear and loathing.
>
> Lance Morrow

WE HAVE LOOKED briefly at some of the current pressures on mothers—the expectation that mother will reject the housewife's role and find her personal fulfillment in a career, and the expectation that, whether single or married, she will have an active sex life. Since these ideas have been widely accepted, it is important to examine some of the consequences of these expectations in the culture. Is the new lifestyle for mother really working?

Obviously feminism has had a positive influence on women in numerous ways. Thousands of women relish being emancipated from their homes and the limited roles of previous decades. The fact that women increasingly enter the world of work attests to the positive payoff career affords women at a personal level.

Both men and women have achieved a heightened

level of consciousness about sexism in all areas of life. A computer company executive spoke of the fact that he no longer hears men speak of having "her (i.e., the secretary) type it up." Now the executive is told that "the secretary will type the contract." A mother spoke to me about an ongoing battle her twelve-year-old daughter is having with a junior high teacher who admits with glee that he is a "male chauvinist pig." The girl and her mother are readying for a battle with this teacher before the board of education. With the increased awareness of sexism has come heightened self-respect for a number of women.

Betty Friedan states that because women now feel greater self-respect and have greater control over their lives than in earlier years, middle-aged women suffer less from depression and insomnia than they did fifteen or twenty years ago.[1]

Nonetheless, women's thrust for greater independence and equality has its dark side. An article in the *Wall Street Journal* entitled "The Cost of Equality" states that as women's roles become more like men's, so too do their problems. According to federal health officials, one of every three Americans with a drinking problem is a woman, as compared with one of six a decade ago.

"From 1965 to 1978, while the percentage of adult men who smoke was dropping from more than half to just 37%, the figure for women held almost unchanged at about 30%. Lung cancer in women is increasing so rapidly that it is estimated that by the mid-eighties it will overtake breast cancer as 'their leading cancer killer.'"

Although twice as many men as women kill themselves, women have become more serious about suicide. No longer do they take overdoses with the possibility of being revived; now they kill themselves by the methods historically used by men—"hanging, gunshots and deliberate car crashes."

Women are increasingly involved in property crimes

such as embezzlement, fraud, and forgery. While in 1960 only one of every six Americans arrested for larceny and theft was a woman, today the figure is one out of three. The *Wall Street Journal* indicates that "employed, middle-class women have contributed disproportionately to the increase of women in crime over the past decade." The article suggests that women who work have more opportunities to steal.

In addition, the article states that working wives have role conflicts the housewife just does not have. A 1977 Rand Corporation study found that working wives have more problems with alcohol than either housewives or single employed women. Paula Johnson, a UCLA research psychologist who worked on this particular study, states that "working wives face role conflicts. They encounter stresses from both work and their husbands to play those (different) roles right."[2]

We do not have to read at great length to learn of the tensions that exist between men and women today. Numerous articles have dealt with the increasing number of men who complain of impotency and other sexual problems. These men cannot handle the aggressive new woman who knows how to achieve her orgasm and expects her lover to provide multiple orgasms with each sexual encounter. Joseph Epstein in *Divorced in America: Marriage in an Age of Possibility* writes of the bedroom olympics that occur regularly in some homes. This pressure to perform sexually does little except generate enmity between the sexes.

And what about the growing distance that exists between mothers and their young? In a *Time* essay entitled "Wondering If Children Are Necessary," Lance Morrow refers to columnist Ann Landers' poll of American parents in which 50,000 responded and 70 percent said that if they had it to do over again, they would never have children. Morrow also mentions author Betty Rollin's choice one-line attack on motherhood: "Who needs it?"

According to Morrow, child abuse is definitely on the rise. More than two million cases are reported per year in America, and police speculate about the instances that go unrecorded.

Additionally, Morrow writes, child pornography flourishes. "In Los Angeles the police estimate that 30,000 children, many of them under the age of five, are used each year as objects of pornography. A number of them are actually sold or rented for that purpose by their parents."

Why have these trends emerged full-blown on the national scene? Morrow states that the self-absorption of the seventies implies a "corollary lack of interest in children."[3] It is difficult to be totally involved in the cult of self and at the same time effectively care for the children who live with us. While this narcissism may be helping mother find gratification outside of home, husband, and children, her children are paying a price for this emphasis on "doing one's own thing."

According to an article by Jim Jerome in the *New York Times Magazine,* the number of suicides among children ten to fourteen years of age has risen 32 percent since 1968. "This trend becomes more ominous in light of the soaring rates of alcohol and drug abuse, criminal offenses and suicide among teenagers." Suicide is now the third leading cause of death (after accidents and homicides) in the 15–24 age group also. Suicides . . . more than doubled among young adults aged 20–24 between 1968 and 1976," states Jerome. "There has been an undeniable increase in self-destructive behavior among youths in America." The article continues: "The message is all too clear: America is producing a lot of depressed young people."[4]

When the second boy in a year (one a ninth grader and one an eleventh grader) attempted suicide in my community, I called the principal of the local high school both had attended. Concerned about what I was reading and learning about youth, I asked Herbert Orell if I could interview him, and he graciously assented.

Having been in education for thirty-three years, Orell could speak authoritatively about young people and trends. He felt that the sixties, with its emphasis on revolt and rebellion, left many young people with an inner vacuum. No longer able to trust established authority or even their own parents, youth searched for anything to fill the void, the inner emptiness—hard rock, drugs, early sexual experiences.

Kids today, stated Orell, are searching for something to live for, but they are having a tremendous struggle finding answers. "We no longer have the support structures in the culture that existed when I was growing up. How many families in this area or in the country have a strong church affiliation? No longer does the family look to the local church for support, and the immediate family is failing to provide youth with the emotional support needed.

"When you consider the rising incidence of single-parent homes and homes where both parents work full-time, many of my students go home daily to empty houses. Home is little more than a bedroom and a place to hang their clothes. Where are the parents? Both feel they must work to support a particular lifestyle—in this community, an upper middle class lifestyle—and after work, many are into narcissism. It is, however, hard to 'do your own thing' and raise children well."

After this sober interview, I talked with Mr. Norman Amend, a guidance counselor at the same high school who has worked with students for more than fourteen years. I asked him for his impression of the stresses that young people face today.

Amend replied, "In talking with other guidance counselors, [I find that] the consensus of opinion is that the severity of adolescents' problems is definitely on the rise. The inner anguish of the modern youth is more severe and affects more young people than ever before. There is a lack of an inner core or much less self-identity among teen-agers today. Kids do not seem to know who they are, and the people who used to flesh out their identities, their parents, live by an entirely different value system than their children. So the chasm between parent and child is great indeed.

"Why this increase in the severity of emotional problems? Just look at our society. We have more single-parent homes, more homes where both parents work full-time and the child is without parental interaction and supervision for most of the day. This creates a child who is driven to peers for any values. Kids who come to my office reveal an emptiness in their lives—a lack of love, a lack of spiritual values, a lack of discipline. That old security is gone, that security fostered by discipline and the presence of at least one adult who supervised activities. It is all permissiveness now, and the kids aren't handling it well."

As I left the local high school that day, I concluded that young people are struggling to find meaning in a world that is basically not very helpful. According to both the principal and the guidance counselor, young people get too little help from their busy and emotionally inaccessible parents as they attempt to flesh out an identity and find something to live for. Some live daily with an inner emptiness that leads to depression and inner angst. For an increasing number, suicide flows out of this inner void.

This brings us back to our original question. Is mother's new lifestyle working for her and for her family? On balance, the evidence indicates that it is not working well at all. Not only has mother's life become more stressful, but tensions with her spouse have increased. And her children?

While we cannot lay the ominous evidence at mother's door alone, nonetheless she is one of the two parents responsible for rearing her children. And since most mothers wish to rear reasonably whole children, it is wise for them to examine all the ramifications of women's new lifestyles. . . .

Is the payoff what some mothers expected it to be?

Is the price too high?

---

[1]Joann S. Lublin, "The Cost of Equality," *Wall Street Journal* (January 14, 1980), p. 1.

[2]Ibid.

[3]Lance Morrow, "Wondering If Children Are Necessary," *Time* (March 5, 1979), p. 42.

[4]Jim Jerome, "Catching Them Before Suicide," *New York Times Magazine* (January 14, 1979), p. 30.

HOW IMPORTANT IS MOTHER?

8

Can Anyone Mother?

The young child's hunger for his mother's love and presence is as great as his hunger for food.

John Bowlby

Dear Mommy, I love you very much. What would I do without you?

a note from ten-year-old Kristen

IN THE EARLIER chapters of this book we looked at some of the current cultural ideas about mothering and questioned both their validity and the results of their application in our society. Now let's try to assess the importance of mother and her role in her child's life. We'll begin by asking two significant questions: How important is mother to her child? and Can anyone mother?

Dr. Jack Raskin, child psychiatrist at Children's Orthopedic Hospital and at the University of Washington in Seattle, believes that the key to healthy personality development lies in the "child's close, unbroken attachment in the early months to people who care for him. Too much disruption of this imbeds in the personality traits that can be destructive for a lifetime."[1]

Dr. Raskin states that depression and emotional deprivation grow out of inadequate affection, poor attachment, and inadequate contact between the child and his caretaker during those early months of life. This depression, in turn, is the root of the problems some individuals have all their lives and may lead to the adolescent problems of drug abuse, pregnancy, suicide, and cult participation. "Depression is knowing inside: 'I am worthless, unloved, unwanted. Nothing will ever be good.'"

Raskin believes that no psychological event is as important as the bonding that occurs between mother and child in the first moments of the child's life. Then, a "beautiful ballet begins to unfold, as the mother gets in tune with her child through the days and weeks." Dr. Raskin feels that fathers, too, form attachment to their babies and that this maternal and paternal attachment becomes the basis for healthy personality growth.[2]

Just what is meant by the term "attachment"? Psychoanalyst John Bowlby, famous for his studies of the mother-child bond, writes of this attachment as the strong tie that forms between the mother figure and the child within the first twelve months of the infant's life. Bowlby points out that this attachment to the mother figure is the child's first human relationship and is the "foundation stone of his personality." This strong attachment to the mother or mother substitute persists until the child reaches his third birthday; after that, proximity to mother is less urgent.[3]

Bowlby notes that attachment behavior is evident in a child throughout latency and only grows weaker during adolescence when other adults become important in the child's life. And then? For most of us, that bond to parents continues into adulthood and only lessens in old age when we attach to the younger generation.

Since mother is so important to her young child, when she leaves temporarily he will become distressed and cry. Upon her return, the child will greet her with "crows of delight."[4]

When mother's absence is permanent, it is a different matter. Since World War II such eminent figures as Anna Freud, Dorothy Burlingham, René Spitz, and John Bowlby have conducted studies of institutionalized children or children who have experienced a succession of foster homes. These studies show that such children are permanently impaired.[5] Some of the children in the studies conducted by Spitz deteriorated "to the mental level of imbeciles at the end of the second year and showed no response to the appearance of a human figure. The motion picture made of the mute, solemn children, lying stuporous in their cribs, is one of the little known horror films of our time."[6]

These studies indicate that the mother figure is crucial in the young child's life. It is, says writer Maggie Scarf in *Unfinished Business,* as if babies are "biologically preprogramed for loving" and mothers are, on their part, ready "to fall in love with their newborns. Such is nature's lovely synchrony." When this relationship is disturbed during the child's first four or five years of life and mother is absent for an extended period of time, the child experiences acute psychological pain. This anguish has three distinct stages: protest, despair, and, finally, detachment. When the child reaches this last stage, Scarf notes, he no longer cares. And if the separation from mother is too long, the process may never be reversed. Some children literally die from the absence of this protective and absorbing emotional bond.[7]

But what, if anything, do these studies of institutionalized children and children who have experienced a succession of foster homes portend for the millions of working mothers who have young children? Can these studies of severely deprived children be applied to children whose mothers leave them at day-care centers for ten to twelve hours each day? Selma Fraiberg, professor of child psychoanalysis at the University of Michigan, does just this in her book *Every Child's Birthright: In Defense of Mothering*.

> A baby who is stored like a package with the neighbors while his mother works may come to know as many indifferent caretakers as a baby in the lowest grade institution and, at the age of one or two years, can resemble in all significant ways the emotionally deprived babies of such an institution.[8]

Mothers of children three and under, according to Fraiberg, need to be with their child most of the time. From three to six years, the child can tolerate mother's absence for a half day. Even then, three to six-year-olds do not profit from, or tolerate well, ten to twelve hours of separation from mother each day.

> When a child spends 11 or 12 hours of his waking day in the care of indifferent custodians, no parent and no educator can say that the child's development is being promoted or enhanced, and common sense tells us that children are harmed by indifference.[9]

While Raskin does not say that mother's working will impair her child's psychological health, he does indicate that working may not give mother enough time to hold, fondle, and interact with her young child.

> Going to work does not necessarily mean bonding is going to be poor, but it does increase the risk, because diminished time is available, and there are other pressures and stresses for the parent.[10]

He suggests that a mother stay home with her child until bonding is solid at two or three, and then if the mother notices that her child is not developing on schedule, she should be willing to modify her work schedule.[11]

There is evidence that some working mothers are not able to handle both job stress and their young children's needs. An article by Susan Muenchow, entitled "Your Baby's Inner Strength", states that emergency-room physicians are noticing not only an increase in child abuse but also an equally life-threatening condition called "failure to thrive"; this means that the child is not receiving enough love to grow.

Muenchow's article points out that children fail to thrive as a result of stresses in parents' lives: marital disruption, job stress, and grinding economic pressure. Because more mothers, as well as fathers, are working in the marketplace, "the 9 to 5 mentality is encroaching more and more into both parents' approach to family life. For many, family relationships have begun to take on the quality of business transactions."[12]

Ironically, while some mothers do not realize how important they are to their young, subhuman primates are programed to be nurturing mothers. Bowlby writes that the chimpanzee, the gorilla, the baboon, and the rhesus macaque keep their infants close to them. The infants sleep beside their mothers at night and never wander far from their sight during the day. They run to their mothers if they become alarmed or afraid. Primate infants, studies show, spend the whole of their infancy in close proximity to their mothers.[13]

Subhuman primates apparently make good mothers. Not only do they stay close to their infants, but when they discipline their young, their "rebuffs were always gentle." And as the offspring grow older and move away from mother, their mothers do not reject or mistreat them.[14]

Baroness Jane Van Lawick-Goodall spent years studying chimpanzee behavior, and when her first child, Grub, was born, she modeled her mothering after the mothering she had observed among female chimps. Says Goodall:

> The female chimp is a good mother. She never leaves her young children or neglects them. I've tried to follow this with Grub. I didn't leave him at all when he was small and I've never left him screaming. I know lots of mothers leave their children alone, but I didn't believe in it. Because I've always been with him, Grub has felt secure right from the beginning. Now he'll wander off on his own quite confidently and he's never gone through the stage of being worried by strangers.[15]

Few mothers can echo Goodall and state that they have never left their children screaming. And yet the question must be asked: What would happen to our young children's sense of security if we kept them close to us during infancy and early childhood? Would we enrich their inner lives in ways we cannot fathom?

CAN ANYONE MOTHER OUR CHILDREN?

In spite of the work done by Bowlby, Goodall and others, not all child development experts believe mother is that important to her young child. Dr. Rudolph Schaeffer, professor of psychology at the University of Strathclyde in Glasgow, states that the baby attaches to numerous people and does not need an exclusive and powerful relationship with mother. Schaeffer does admit, however, that a child needs a "limited range of familiar people who will provide the child with consistency of care throughout the years of his childhood." While a mother is influential in her child's development, so too, writes Schaeffer, are older siblings and the neighbor next door.[16]

Dr. Urie Bronfenbrenner, professor of human development at Cornell University, offers a similar point of view. Bronfenbrenner states that even very young children can function adequately with good surrogate care. He notes that cross-cultural studies do not support the idea that a child must be cared for by his mother. Men,

Bronfenbrenner contends, are just as adept as women in caring for children, since "it's the children, you know, who teach us to care for them."[17]

At the same time, Bronfenbrenner qualifies his remarks by adding that each child needs someone to make an irrational commitment to him. By this, Bronfenbrenner means someone who will not pack up and go home at five o'clock. Additionally, this caretaker must love the child better than other people's children and the child must return the love. Or, to put it another way, "the child should spend a substantial amount of time with somebody who's crazy about him."

It is thus okay if a person other than mother rears the child so long as this caretaker has an "irrational involvement" with that child, thinks the child is more important than other people's children, loves the child dearly, and is trusted enough to be loved in return.[18] Somehow, this caretaker sounds suspiciously like a mother.

WHO WILL MOTHER THE CHILDREN?

While some mothers may breathe a sigh of relief when they read experts who assert that anyone can mother their children, other mothers will feel that this assertion damages their self-esteem and robs them of one of their basic reasons for being. Historically, many women have derived deep feelings of gratification from the nurturing process. To say that anyone can mother or, more accurately, that someone else will do a better job than the child's biological or psychological mother is to cut away at the root of one of life's most basic relationships.

But even if anyone can mother our children, (and some mothers will never assent to this) the next question becomes: *Who* will mother the young?

Feminist literature occasionally drafts fathers to mother children. Why not have men quit their jobs or at least spend equal time mothering children since women have borne the burden of child care through the ages? And increasingly we read of fathers who either stay home with their children while their wives function as breadwinners or at least give tacit approval, and some time and effort, to the idea.

One such father is sociologist S. M. Miller. In a delightful essay Miller speaks frankly of his liberated marriage and his attempt to participate in housewifery and child care.[19] He, an ardent feminist, is brother, son, and husband of working women. Married to a physician whose career aspirations he endorsed, Miller set out to become an equal partner with his wife in the truest sense. Miller found, however, that he resented housewifery and left the running of the household to his wife, who subordinated her career once children were born. While he desired to co-parent equally, Miller discovered that his wife became the children's psychological parent.

Miller feels uneasy about this and writes, "She is now realizing fuller professional development. I have always felt guilty about her not achieving more"; and he castigates himself for not being more involved with his children's lives. What went wrong? He asks:

> Where is the egalitarian family life one would reasonably expect from my sophistication about women's lib issues and my personal experience with them in my younger manhood?[20]

Miller offers no definitive answer, though his thoughtful article resonates with a kind of bittersweet sadness. He even wonders if he married a career-minded woman because he did not think so well of himself that he could have lived with the "(overwhelming) devotion" that an "easily giving or male-centered" woman might have given him.

Few fathers are as willing as S. M. Miller to share in

the tasks of housewifery and child-rearing. Many men still enjoy leaving the wife in charge when they go to work in the morning. For women married to such traditionalists, the most likely source of child care then becomes the day-care center.

This could be an optimum solution if all day-care centers had excellent facilities and warm, loving, educated personnel. Some few do; many do not. A national survey conducted by the National Council of Jewish Women found that only about one center in four provided quality day-care service that included attention to the children's physical, intellectual, and personality development. Most of the rest provided baby-sitting, and the worst were lacking even in that.[21] In the meantime, millions of mothers drop their pre-school children off at any local facility which will take them and hope for the best.

So if we denigrate mother's role in her child's life and substitute father, only to find that he will not stand in the breach, and if we are unhappy with the quality of day-care available, we are left to find whomever we can to rear our children. And sometimes, though we know how critical the child's caretaker ultimately is, we end up asking a stranger to shape our child's humanity.

Mothers, one just might conclude, are difficult to replace.

---

[1]Dale Mills, "To Work or Not to Work After the Baby Comes," *Seattle Times Magazine* (July 1, 1979), p. 8.
[2]Ibid.
[3]John Bowlby, *Attachment*, vol. 1 (New York: Basic Books, 1969), pp. 204–205.
[4]Ibid., p. 200.
[5]Selma Fraiberg, *Every Child's Birthright: In Defense of Mothering* (New York: Bantam Books, 1977), pp. 58–59.
[6]Ibid., p. 60.
[7]Scarf, *Unfinished Business*, pp. 74–77.
[8]Fraiberg, *Child's Birthright*, p. 61.
[9]Ibid., p. 102.
[10]Mills, "To Work Or Not To Work After the Baby Comes," p. 9.
[11]Ibid, p. 8.

[11]Mills, "To Work or Not," p. 8.
[12]Susan Muenchow, "Your Baby's Inner Strength," *Parents' Magazine* (March, 1980), p. 51.
[13]Bowlby, *Attachment,* p. 184.
[14]Ibid., p. 192.
[15]Timothy Green, *The Restless Spirit* (New York: Walker and Co., 1970), p. 12.
[16]Rudolph Schaeffer, *Mothering* (Cambridge, Mass.: Harvard University Press, 1977), p. 107.
[17]Susan Byrne, "Nobody Home: The Erosion of the American Family," *Psychology Today* (May, 1977), p. 45.
[18]Ibid., p. 43.
[19]S. M. Miller, "On Men: The Making of a Confused Middle Class Husband," *Social Policy* (July/August, 1971) 2.2, pp. 33–39.
[20]Ibid., p. 34.
[21]Olds, *Mother Who Works,* p. 35.

9

Lost Mothers

> I guess I don't know very much about my mother. She was an alcoholic who early on gave me to someone else to raise. You might say I never had a mother.
>
> a thirty-year-old male

DURING THE PAST several years I have encountered numerous people in literature and life who have, for one reason or another, lost their mothers in early childhood.

I have been touched by the poignancy and the pain so apparent in these individuals as they have spoken of their mothers. One man in his seventies whose mother died in childbirth never found an adequate surrogate mother. He confessed, "I never had a mother," in somber tones as if his whole life had been irrevocably colored by that fact.

One of the most poignant literary statements about the importance of a mother who is lost to death is contained in the book *Hannah's Daughters* by Dorothy Gallagher. This is the story of six generations of Washington State women who range in age from 97 to 2. Hannah, who is 97, is the most touching of all.

Hannah's mother died when Hannah was three, and her father then took her to his mother's farm to live. Although the grandmother took care of Hannah's physical needs, she could not or would not give the child affection. Hannah speaks of their relationship:

> Oh, my grandma was good to me, if leaving a kid wander alone all over the place is good. I had the very best of clothing, the very best of eats. But no love, and that's what I wanted. If they loved me, they didn't let me know it. Oh, my daddy loved me, but I didn't see him. Not once a year hardly. He was always in the north woods, working.[1]

While her grandmother did not give Hannah love and affection, she did discipline Hannah. Once when Hannah used some writing paper and colored pencils that belonged to a hired girl, the grandmother tied her to a bedpost for hours. On another occasion, Hannah broke a comb on purpose and her grandmother took her to a barber and had all her long blond hair cut off. Hannah came home looking like a boy. Through the years, Hannah, by her own account, learned to be good, but she felt an emptiness inside.

Hannah lived with her grandmother until she married a man she thought would enlarge her life. "I thought I'd have someone to care for me." She hoped Earl would help her eradicate her inner loneliness, but instead he left Hannah for another woman.

When Earl left, Hannah did not even have salt in the house. She returned home to live on her father's farm as the Widow Lambertson, bringing with her two children, a boy and a girl. Hannah said that she never played with her children because she simply did not feel comfortable with small children. She had not known a "joyous time" growing up herself and knew little to do other than dutifully care for her children's physical needs.

After a period of time Hannah married again, a man named Matt who worked as a day laborer. Matt was good to Hannah and they lived together until he died. Some time later Hannah married again. She married Tom Nesbitt for companionship but had "more companionship from a cat than I got from him. He never talked. He sat there just like he was lost, lost in his own dreams, I guess, I don't know." Although Tom was not easy to live with, Hannah remained with him until he died.

Finally one winter day near the end of her long life, Hannah asked God about that inner longing, the longing that drove her into successive marriages. "'God,' I prayed, 'is that longing for my mother?' I named it and He took it away. I haven't had it since. That awful hurting, that longing. That's what led me to marriage. But my husbands never touched that longing."[2]

MOTHER LONGING

I grew up living with a woman who had a similar longing for a mother long since dead. Mother was only four when her mother died. Recently she described her mother's dying as a sad and poignant event. Mother remembers standing outside the bedroom door, peering in at her mother who lay in bed surrounded by a husband and two physicians. Their somber tones alerted mother to the seriousness of her mother's condition. Within hours my grandmother, a woman who bore eight children, died, and her death ushered in an emotionally impoverished childhood for my mother.

On the day she spoke of her mother's dying, my mother painted a picture of herself as an emotionally neglected child. No one apparently helped her work through her grief or even gave her any special attention. "I cried alot for weeks after mother died, but went off by myself to do it." Mother spoke of taking flowers from her yard to her mother's grave, and this apparently comforted her.

If English psychoanalyst John Bowlby is correct, then my mother experienced a devastating loss when my grandmother died. Like Hannah, mother found it difficult to express affection because she received so little in her early life. "I can only remember sitting on my father's lap once after my mother died," she said. Most likely, her unsuccessful father, a man who later lost his farm, was overwhelmed by his own grief and the prospect of parenting his large family alone.

Her father remarried, true. But the woman who came home as stepmother was unable to love and shelter his brood. Very quickly she bore her own children to love, and these two boys received her care while the others were onlookers to this domestic drama. I knew her as prim-mouthed Grandma Mary who refused to give me even one flower from her prolific and gorgeous garden.

Grandma Mary never touched mother's inner core; she was no warm surrogate mother. Instead, mother grew up, in most respects, a motherless child who idealized the woman who bore her. How she loved to talk about Martha Callie Bradford whose family consisted of fine, prosperous merchants. Even in our deepest poverty, mother, who identified with her deceased mother rather than her living father, walked tall and strove to rise above our circumstances.

Mother's favorite poem was one she memorized in high school and loved to recite to me. A sentimental rhyme called "Somebody's Mother," this poem written by Mary Dow Brine speaks of an old woman who is helped across the street on a cold, wintry day by a young gallant. The woman in the poem is an ephemeral being just as my deceased grandmother must have been to my mother. Yet the key is the fact that the woman is *somebody's mother*, and for a woman who received too little mothering, how central a concept this. It touched a fire that burned inside my mother's heart, a longing that has never been extinguished.

My own life has also been greatly affected by the death of my maternal grandmother. Her death meant that mother's maternal cup, though never empty, was never very full. Since mother had so few years of mothering, she has had difficulty in forming close relationships with others, especially her children. When we come close, she, who seemingly cannot tolerate intimacy, pushes us away. And so the pattern has continued throughout our lives, creating no little pain and sadness for my sister and for me. We who found surrogate mothers as we grew up would warm our mother by our maternal fire, but for the present, this is not to be. And each time I see her, I realize anew just how much mother's life has been shaped by the loss of a loving, caring mother.

Writer C. S. Lewis also lost his mother before he became an adolescent. She died of cancer at home while Lewis, knowing she was seriously ill, waited just outside her bedroom. Writing in *Surprised by Joy,* Lewis offers this perspective on the singular importance his mother held in his life:

> With my mother's death all settled happiness, all that was tranquil and reliable, disappeared from my life. There was much fun, many pleasures, many stabs of Joy; but no more of the old security. It was sea and islands now; the great continent had sunk like Atlantis.[3]

Recently, I attended a meeting of ALMA, an organization of adoptees who are searching for their biological mothers, and gained another perspective on the importance of mother to her child. I learned of this organization from a friend who lent me Florence Fisher's book *The Search for Anna Fisher,* an account of the author's own search for her birth mother. Florence Fisher later founded

ALMA and works with the organization today. A college friend invited me to attend an ALMA meeting in her home and I went, curious about these people who work hard to find their birth mothers.

About twelve women came to Pam's house that cold winter night. Most were well-dressed and some were college-educated. Only one man attended the meeting, and his self-designated role was to encourage the women present in their search, even in the face of insurmountable difficulties. He had already found his birth mother.

During the meeting each woman spoke about her search, and while about half were in the process of searching, the other half had already found their mothers.

One woman who was in her mid-thirties and had the slimmest threads of evidence to go on broke down and wept. She who had known love in her adopted home felt driven to find her biological mother and met with resistance at every turn.

Following this account, another woman, in her late twenties, spoke happily of finding her biological mother and a whole new family at the same time. She had searched for a brief time, had been successful in locating her mother, and had been well-received. She spoke of a trip to Florida to visit her mother and of meals with a newly found grandmother, aunts, and uncles in New York City.

This cheery account was followed by a bitter tale about a birth mother in the Midwest who refused to talk to her biological child. The child, a mother herself in her mid-forties, was struggling to deal with this rejection and was finding the process difficult.

At break time I asked the group why they were so avidly searching for their mothers. "Why not fathers?" I queried. The women said that with their mothers at least a hospital record existed. Also, the women felt that because their mothers had carried them in their wombs, some kind of bond had been created.

Most wanted a bond to exist. This lessened the pain of knowing that, for whatever reason, their mothers had given them away. One younger woman spoke with pride about the fact that her mother had cared enough to knit a three-piece outfit for her unborn baby. This woman was wearing this little suit when she arrived at her adoptive parents' home and later used it for her dolls. She had only recently been told the origin of the suit. The other women listened to this account and registered that this suit, this one loving act, had enormous significance for the speaker. Not one of the other women came forth with this kind of evidence of maternal love. Most likely they had none.

As I listened to these women, it became apparent that most had grown up in warm families. They had no desire to hurt their adoptive mothers. "It's just that I have to see if I can locate my birth mother," said one young woman. "I had no desire to find her until my doctor asked for a medical history and I realized I knew nothing about my genetic endowment! Now I am determined to find my mother, for my sake and for my children's. They also need some sense of a personal history."

I was struck by the depth of longing these women had to find and know their birth mothers. All had been given up for adoption within days after birth, yet some mysterious cord tied them to biological mothers never seen, never known. Strange. At a time when the culture denigrates mother with abandon, some women will pursue any lead to find mothers they consider of utmost importance.

How important is mother? No relationship on earth has as much potential for good or ill. No other arms hold us so often during those first hours and months of life as the arms of mother. Cold or loving, rough or tender, those arms give us our first messages about the world we have come to inhabit. Fortunate indeed are those who are born to welcoming, loving mothers.

For those who have lost mothers to death when they were very young, those whose mothers felt they must give them away for someone else to raise, and those whose mothers are too absorbed in their own lives to give the nurture so desperately needed, life is harder.

How important is any mother? Ask her child.

---

[1]Dorothy Gallagher, *Hannah's Daughters: Six Generations of an American Family 1876–1976* (New York: Thomas Crowell, 1976), p. 28.
[2]Ibid., p. 94.
[3]C. S. Lewis, *Surprised by Joy* (New York: Harcourt, Brace and World, Inc., 1955), p. 21.

10

Enlarging Our Vision of Mother

> The virtues of mothers shall be visited on their children.
>
> Charles Dickens

THE BOOK OF Proverbs states that without a vision the people perish. Many mothers in America today are floundering because they lack a vision of the enormous potential of the mothering role. Mired in the negative portrayal of mothers in much feminist literature, an image that holds sway in the media, they need to be encouraged to believe in the positive influence they can have in their children's lives.

One way to gain encouragement is to look to another era to see what people said about mothers. Recently I did just this at the Library of Congress and learned that history has held mothers in high esteem. Ordering up books published in the early 1900s—now long out of print—I was surprised to see the positive portrait of mother that emerged. In volume after volume mother is portrayed as the most powerful influence in her child's life. She is spiritual advisor, earliest teacher, loving nurturer. Mother is, as one writer put it, "a molder of men."

A book published first in the twenties illustrates the theme of mother as teacher. Mable Bartlett and Sophia Baker, writing in the book *Mothers—Makers of Men,* quote numerous famous men as they comment on their mothers' influence on their intellectual lives. French poet Lamartine said this about his mother Alexis Francoise Desroys:

> My education was wholly centered in the glance, more or less serene, and the smile, more or less open, of my mother. The reins of my heart were in her hand.
>
> I drank in, as a plant from the soil, the first nourishing juices of my young intellect from the books carefully selected by my mother. But I drank deep, above all, from my mother's mind; I read through her eyes; I felt through her impressions; I lived through her life.[1]

Abraham Lincoln, on our side of the Atlantic, was another man who stated that he owed much of his intellectual development to the efforts of his mother, Nancy Hanks, who died when her son was ten years old. Not only did Nancy teach young Abe to read, but she walked miles to secure books for him when necessary. She was intent on enlarging his world and encouraged him to rise above the family's stifling poverty. Abraham Lincoln bestowed a bouquet upon his mother years later when he said that she was chiefly responsible for all he was or ever hoped to become.[2]

Another mother-teacher who participated in the education of her son was the Scottish Presbyterian mother of art critic and writer John Ruskin. From an early age, Ruskin stood at his mother's knee, reading and memorizing portions of the Bible.

> My mother's influence in molding my character was conspicuous. She forced me to learn daily long chapters of the Bible by heart. To that discipline and patient, accurate resolve I owe not only much of my general power of taking pains, but the best part of my taste for literature.[3]

As I read the various quotes about mothers as teachers, I was struck by the number of those mothers of achieving children who taught their young from the Bible. Not only did these mothers value the spiritual power of the Scripture, but they obviously found it an effective educational tool as well.

One mother of famous sons, Susanna Wesley, selected the Bible as the first book her children would ever read. Susanna, who had studied Greek, Latin, French, logic, and metaphysics herself, taught her ten (she bore nineteen, but only ten survived infancy, among them John and Charles) children while at the same time she ran an orderly household. Her tactic was to take each child into the schoolroom once he reached the age of five and patiently teach him the alphabet. From there the child plunged into reading the Bible, starting with Genesis 1:1. This mother who functioned as teacher from 9 to 12 and 2 to 5 each day listened patiently while each child spelled out the verses word for word, and she tolerated no interruptions in her teaching schedule.[4]

Any mother who decides to consciously educate her child brings to the task something that no paid educator has to offer: a significant investment in the pupil and a conviction that the child will prosper under her tutelege. A mother knows she cannot quit and go home at the end of the day. Her feelings about her child keep her giving, believing, and teaching for all hours.

Writers Bartlett and Baker give us some insight into how an adult-child viewed his mother's concern. Thomas Edison, who was educated at home by an intelligent and sympathetic mother when she learned that his teachers felt he had inferior ability, had this to say about his mother: "My mother was the making of me. She was so true, so sure of me; and I felt that I had someone to live for, someone I must not disappoint."[5]

History's famous men have not been the only recipients of a mother's concern and teaching. I can cite any number of contemporary women who are unwilling to leave the education of their sons and daughters solely to church and school.

For example, a former college roommate has done more to enrich her family's life and educate her sons than any other woman I have known. Mother of five boys under fourteen, Marty Larson started fostering creativity in her first-born when he was very young. Making her own replicas of the Montessori toys, Marty set aside an hour each morning to read to Eric. Later, when she and her husband, Elliott, went to Afghanistan as missionaries, Marty purchased enough books to educate their toddler through the fifth grade in every important subject. From time to time I hear about the reading she does with each child daily and once received a twelve-page bibliography of books "too good to miss." This mother, who is also a gourmet cook and hospitable woman, uses her abundant energies, in part, to teach her children.

Marty Larson reminds me of another mother who was vitally interested in the development of her children. This woman, Sarah Edwards, lived in New England in the 1700s. Married to the famous clergyman and theologian, Jonathan Edwards, she was mother of eleven children. At the same time, Sarah maintained a vital and intensely loving marriage.

Writing about the Edwards family, author Elizabeth Dodds points out, without apology, that "the way children turn out is always a reflection on their mother." Then she chronicles the prolific social contributions that streamed from the Edwards children and their descendants.

Dodds refers to the study done by A. E. Winship in 1900, in which he lists some of the accomplishments of the 1,400 Edwards descendants he located. The Edwards family produced

13 college presidents
65 professors
100 lawyers and a dean of a law school
30 judges
66 physicians and a dean of a medical school
80 holders of public office
three United States senators
mayors of three large cities
governors of three states
a vice-president of the United States
a controller of the United States Treasury[6]

Winship believed that "much of the capacity and talent, intensity and character, of the more than 1,400 of the Edwards family is due to Mrs. Edwards."

How did Sarah Edwards do it? A deeply Christian woman, Sarah emerges from the pages of Dodds' book as a firm, patient mother who treated her children with courtesy and love. Samuel Hopkins, a contemporary who spent much time in the Edwards' household, said that Sarah was able to guide her children without angry words or blows. Unlike many mothers today, Sarah had only to speak once and her children obeyed her.

> In their manners they were uncommonly respectful to their parents. When their parents came into the room, they all rose instinctively from their seats and never resumed them until their parents were seated.[7]

These children who were so well-treated by their parents in turn treated each other with love and respect.

In her management of her busy colonial household, Sarah puts her modern counterparts to shame. We, who have only to press buttons to start our many machines, can little imagine the sheer physical labor required of the colonial housewife. Sarah had multitudinous jobs: to see that the candles and clothes were made, the food preserved, the garden planted, the fire stoked, and the guests fed and comfortably housed. Contiguously, she taught her children to work and to deal with life.

A psychologist in her own right, Sarah

> . . . carefully observed the first appearance of resentment and illwill in her young children, towards any person whatever, and did not connive at it . . . but was careful to show her displeasure and suppress it to the utmost; yet not by angry, wrathful words, which often provoke children to wrath. . . . Her system of discipline was begun at a very early age and it was her rule to resist the first, as well as every subsequent exhibition of temper or disobedience in the child . . . wisely reflecting that until a child will obey his parents he will never be brought to obey God.[8]

As a disciplinarian Sarah made her requirements perfectly clear to her children and tolerated no misbehavior. The result was a household that emanated love and harmony.

Last year my daughter Holly showed me an excerpt from Esther Edwards' diary, in which she described her home as an aviary. Mother and daughters sang praise to God from different parts of the house, blending sounds that wafted heavenward. I thought at the time that this was a beautiful image to use to describe the emotional climate of a household. What joy must have permeated that family's life on occasion!

As Elizabeth Dodds makes abundantly clear in her book, a mother is not merely rearing her one, two, or four children. She is also affecting future generations for good or ill. All the love, nurture, education, and character-building that spring from mother work their alchemy on the psyches of those sons and daughters. The results show up in the children's accomplishments, attitudes toward life, and parenting capacity. It was, after all, one of Sarah Edwards' grandsons, Timothy Dwight, president of Yale, who (echoing Lincoln) said of his mother, Mary: "All that I am and all that I shall be, I owe to my mother."[9]

As one ponders this praise given his mother by one of history's achievers, the question arises: Are we women unhappy in our mothering role because we make too little, rather than too much, of that role? Do we see what we have to give our children as minor rather than major and, consequently, send them into the world without a strong core identity and strong spiritual values?

It was the great investment of time that mothers like Sarah Edwards and Susanna Wesley made in the lives of their children that garnered such high praise. One doesn't teach a child to read in an hour or stretch a child's mind in a few days.

Have we as mothers unwisely left the education of our children to school and church, believing that we can fill in around the edges? And would we feel better about ourselves if we were more actively involved in the teaching of our children?

I think so.

A thread runs throughout the whole of life: Only as we invest much will the yield be great. Our children are growing up in a rough, tough world, and they need us to invest much time and energy in their lives. Only then will they—and we—experience significant gain.

Given the vision of a mother's critical importance to her growing children, how should we order our lives?

WHERE HAVE ALL THE MOTHERS GONE?

[1]Mabel Bartlett and Sophia Baker, *Mothers—Makers of Men* (New York: Exposition Press, 1952), p. 44.
[2]Louis M. Notkin, ed., *Mother Tributes from the World's Great Literature* (New York: Samuel Curl, 1943), p. 117.
[3]Ibid., p. 144.
[4]Bartlett and Baker, *Makers of Men*, pp. 66–68.
[5]Ibid., p. 92.
[6]Elizabeth D. Dodds, *Marriage to a Difficult Man* (Philadelphia, Pa., 1971), p. 38.
[7]Ibid., p. 43.
[8]Ibid.
[9]Ibid., p. 209.

WHERE DO WE GO FROM HERE?

11

If Mother Must Work

> If you write a book about mothers, don't try to titillate our guilt. Some of us are trapped in jobs that we cannot leave while at the same time we know that we don't have enough time for our children. Lots of us already feel guilty.
>
> a full-time working mother

UNLIKE MUCH OF the literature written for and about women today, this book has not focused entirely on mother and her needs for fulfillment. Equally important has been the child's need for effective mothering during the years he lives at home.

This focus has been intentional. The culture has stressed women's needs for more than a decade with little regard for their children. The underlying assumption is that children will fare well enough at their day-care centers or with the baby-sitter. The focus of popular literature is on mother's salary, career advancement, "fun," and escape from the boredom of life at home. So positive is the portrait of the working mother that many women feel they *must* work outside the home.

In addition to those women who feel they must work

for reasons of self-esteem are those millions of mothers who have concluded they must work to make ends meet. These women are either heads of households due to divorce or a spouse's death and are therefore responsible for most of the earned income or they are wives supplementing a husband's income.

Possibly no one fits the "mother who must work for economic reasons" category better than the separated or divorced mother. Called the "new poor," the divorced mother and her children nearly always experience a radical change in lifestyle after the husband and father leaves home. Even if her estranged husband regularly pays child support (and statistics say that relatively few do), the separated or divorced mother often feels that she must work.

Increasingly, married women find that inflation has eroded their family's buying power, and they too join the "must work for economic reasons" category. One family I interviewed concluded that they simply could not live on father's income alone. Although Jim earns nearly twenty thousand dollars in his middle-management job, he supports a wife, three children, two cars, and a house payment. Feeling strapped, he encouraged his wife, a high school graduate, to work full-time. Yet even with her additional earnings, the family continues to struggle.

When a family is confronted with financial need, the easiest solution is for mother to seek full-time employment. The reasons are obvious: part-time work is confined to low-level jobs, pays poorly, is hard to find. Employers prefer women who will make a full-time commitment to their work. Full-time employment "feels" safer or more permanent, and full benefits come only with full-time work.

But what if children need significantly more mothering than their harried working mothers can give? And what if, as psychoanalyst Selma Fraiberg states, the child needs mother most of the day until the age of three, and for half a day until school starts? What is the mother to do who must earn money?

This is not an easy question to answer. There may well be situations in which a full-time job is the only alternative. Before we too readily accept full-time employment as the only viable option, however, I want to share some other possibilities which have worked for me and for numerous other women as well.

One alternative is for mother to find or create a job that she can do at home while her children are young and during school hours when they are older.

The book *Women Working Home*, by Marion Behr and Wendy Lazar, states that thousands of women are discovering that it "is possible to remain at home and establish profitable enterprises that have an impact upon the mainstream of American economic life."[1] Bureau of Labor Statistics indicate that in 1979 some 1.9 million women in the United States were self-employed—a 43 percent increase since 1972. Additionally, in 1977 there were 702,000 women-owned businesses in this country and about half were conducted from the home. "Those businesses accounted for $41.5 billion in receipts and represent a 30% increase in women-owned firms and a 72% increase in receipts since 1972."[2]

Why are so many women choosing to work at home? Behr and Lazar cite some of the more obvious reasons: proximity to children, desire to avoid commuting, the need for additional income, flexibility, and the low cost of operating a home-based business. An advertising consultant is quoted as saying:

> I work at home because it pays better, because I have more freedom creatively, because there is some flexibility in scheduling time for working, and because I find satisfaction in the self-discipline working at home demands. I feel that, by building up my own

> at-home business, I will have found a perfect . . . way of blending career and motherhood when we have children. I believe . . . I can work it out to have the best of both worlds.[3]

In addition to the good feelings the contributors to *Women Working Home* mentioned—the satisfaction of watching one's business grow, learning to handle failure, and developing greater self-confidence—one great reward for working at home is that "home is where the kids are." Mothers who feel that their presence is important for their children's well-being are glad to be able to work at home. A divorced jewelry manufacturer works at home because she seldom saw her mother when she was growing up and she doesn't want her children to have a similar experience. A theater coach works at home because she feels no baby-sitter can rival her "mother's touch." And an attorney has a home-based office so that she is on location if her children need her to buttress their self-esteem.[4]

Women who opt for a home-based business pursue widely different routes. Some engage in traditional occupations and offer either child-care, catering, or house-cleaning services. Others sell their crafts or custom-made clothes. Still others market their skills as piano, baton, or dance instructors. Another group of women use skills honed in the corporate world to support their own public relations, advertising, investment, or marketing firms.

Women Working Home lists occupations that range from collection agent to artist to horticulturalist. Sometimes women choose to start an unusual business, as did Madeleine Fink and Emily Rosen, founders of Witty Ditty, a personalized singing telegram service. Using their backgrounds as verse writers and producers of amateur shows, Fink and Rosen have written "telegrams for movie stars, TV personalities, rock groups, bank presidents, executives of every description, and lovelorn teenagers."[5]

No composer of singing telegrams, I started a more usual home-based business when I returned to the United States after two years in England. And I might never have thought of becoming my own boss if I had located that ideal part-time job I tried for weeks to find. When a friend of mine learned that I had found nothing to supplement my monthly support check, he suggested that I start a business as an editorial consultant, utilizing skills acquired from years of teaching English. Armed with a three-dollar business license and an offer of a first writing assignment, I followed his advice.

At first I wrote a quarterly journal which dealt with criminal justice issues, and then, as news of my skills spread by word of mouth, more opportunities opened up. Soon I was writing for a major insurance company, a group of economists, and a public relations firm.

When I first started my business, I charged five dollars an hour and worked about four hours a day. Later I increased my fee to fifteen dollars an hour and found that I earned as much or more in half the time as I had formerly earned teaching. In addition, I honed writing skills, and the editing eventually led to the publication of my first book.

There are, of course, risks associated with having one's own business. For the woman who has never thought of having her own firm, the prospect of trying to earn a living by marketing her skills can be frightening. When I, a former teacher, began producing newsletters and journals with no experience in layout, I was often afraid. What if I made mistakes? Well, I did. Lots. One journal even had to be printed twice. But as I persevered, earned my fees, and paid my taxes, my self-confidence grew.

Besides, nothing in life is without risk. While a job with a corporation may feel safer than a home-based business, no job is ultimately secure. Bosses do fire employees, and some businesses go bankrupt. And all the while a mother is commuting and working long hours away from home, she is taking some risk with her children's psychological welfare. That may, in the final analysis, be the greater risk.

Women who use their gifts or hobbies to create their own businesses are among the most satisfied working mothers I know. They have some control over their time and can be there if their children need them. When I had my own business, if one of the children was sick, I stayed home. Or if we wanted to visit friends in San Francisco, I scheduled the publication of the newsletter or journal so that I could take a four-day weekend.

To have a home-based business and earn enough to make ends meet brings much gratification. To have that business grow and flourish is exciting. One woman who started her business in her basement flat and now has exclusive shops in London, Tokyo, New York, Milan, and Melbourne, among other places, is Laura Ashley. Working with her husband Bernard, Laura began by printing designs on fabric which was later made into towels and napkins and sold in London shops. Although the business started slowly in 1953, the couple now run fourteen factories and sales are at $100 million.[6] Laura Ashley's "romantic look" in women's fashions as well as her wallpaper and fabric designs are highly prized by many women throughout the world.

Of course, few will go from kitchen table to multimillion dollar business. Most women will have moderate expectations and returns, like Christine, whose husband left her with three small boys under eight. Although she considered taking a full-time job, Christine chose instead to start her own business cleaning house because she could keep her toddler with her. Earning almost ten dollars an hour, Christine was able to supplement the child support her husband sent her. And when her youngest was older and could handle her absence for part of the day, she found a part-time job in a local hospital where she now works as an assistant occupational therapist.

For the mother who wishes an alternative to running her own business or working full-time, job sharing is a possibility. In an article entitled "Working Parents—1981 Style," authors Muenchow and Biddle write of the present trend toward job sharing in business. "Unlike many forms of part-time work, job sharing, while far from widespread, is gaining acceptance in relatively high paying, high prestige occupations." The writers mention a Stanford University study of 240 job sharers nationwide. Half were teachers and administrators; the remainder included counselors, researchers, editors, and librarians.[7]

Whatever job she takes or creates, the mother who is a Christian must look at the issue of the working mother from a different perspective than her non-Christian counterpart. Basically, she has to deal with biblical attitudes toward money and realize that it is far more important to God that her priorities are right than that she ever earn much money.

For the Christian, money is never to be the first priority in life. In Hebrews we read that God will never abandon us; therefore, we should be content with what we have. Scripture is full of promises of provision for the believer. We need only to trust God as Father and administer properly the goods that we have been given. We read:

> Bring the whole tithe into the storehouse, that there may be food in my house. Test me in this, says the Lord Almighty, and see if I will not throw open the floodgates of heaven and pour out so much blessing that you will not have room enough for it (Mal. 3:10 NIV).

My husband Don and I have experienced the reality of this verse. But we learned to give not from the easy stance of affluence but from the grinding position of poverty. It happened this way. Within two years after our marriage, Don lost his job and was unemployed for four frightening months. When he finally found another position, we were dismayed to learn that he would earn five thousand dollars less than in his previous job.

During this stressful period of our lives, I considered full-time employment, but finally elected to teach part-time at a local university so that I could be home with the girls after school. I earned little, but Don supported me in this decision because he believed my mother-presence was important to Holly and Kristen. To help us out of our tension and worry, God sent a marvelous man into our lives to teach us about God's monetary principle. In short, Adger McKay gave us a crash course entitled "How to Always Have Enough."

Adger, whose whole life was consistent with his message, shared a vital truth with us at lunch one day. Leaning forward, this man, who along with his sunny wife Ann had been a missionary to Mexico, said: "When a man gives recklessly to God, God will give recklessly to him." Adger and Ann had experienced this in abundance. Adger's favorite saying as he reached for the luncheon check was, "Now I'm going to get the blessing."

Keenly influenced by Adger's teaching and the illustration of his life, Don and I began tithing on Don's gross income. God tested our faith in subsequent months because Don again changed jobs, our bank account went down to zero, and we were for a time without medical insurance. But we were never unable to pay our bills nor were we ever in serious need.

It is now five years since we started tithing. Don has quadrupled his income, we have moved into a house almost triple the value of the one we lived in then, and we have all we need. Not all we want, but as it says in 2 Corinthians: "All that we need for ourselves and every good cause." Moreover, I have confidence in God and do not give in to hysterical fear when unexpected bills arise. We have learned, beginning in our poverty, that if we will obey the Father, He will provide for us.

I grew so tired of our poverty during that time that I told God I never wanted to worry about money again. I would do my part—give, even recklessly at times—and I would trust Him to do His. To date, He and I have kept this agreement.

Thus far this chapter has addressed the mother who feels she must work for economic reasons. What about the millions of mothers who work for personal fulfillment, women who were basically unhappy at home? These mothers, among whom are those sociologist Jessie Bernard calls "the gifted professionals," feel they are literally wasting their gifts if they stay home; and they tell themselves and others that they are better mothers if they work.

I had a heated discussion this summer with one of these "gifted professionals" who told me with vehemence that she had hated being home with her babies. Moreover, she was certain that she took far better care of *her* children than all those "smother mothers" who lived nearby. With that pronouncement, she made a sweeping gesture with her arm that included most of her neighborhood.

Why do some women hate being at home? If a mother is miserable at home, alone, perhaps she cannot bear to confront her essential, inner self. She may be fleeing herself rather than her children. For the housewife's life is, at base, an encounter with one's insides. It is to see oneself without the facade, stripped, naked. It is to forgo the props, to be deprived of positive societal images. I am no longer teacher, lawyer, or doctor. I am quite simply myself. Surely, housewives just as working mothers, can flee aloneness, but when a woman stops running, she peers into her own soul, and the examination of one's soul is never easy.

If a mother suffers from a painfully low self-image, and I did, then to be deprived of the props that working in the marketplace affords is painful in the extreme. Because of my early life, I felt driven toward accomplishment and felt most alive when I measured up to the expectations of others.

Moreover, even after living as a Christian for years, my values were skewed. I placed great emphasis on earning a salary and on having a ready answer for that destructive question: "What do you *do?*"

Few people are truly concerned about what we are. But God is. And He is out to heal misery and wounded self-esteem. He has shown me that His love is not contingent on anything I produce or the accolades of peers—God loves me as I sit, walk, stand today. It does not matter whether I ever publish another book or pursue a career the culture values or earn significant money. I am okay just as I am. When I finally came to this perception, my old restlessness disappeared. Peace came and has never left me since. The Holy Spirit took that monkey off my back that had driven me toward accomplishment most of my life, and I feel better about my own worth than ever before. And this transformation occurred, not in the marketplace, but during my years at home, writing and mothering my children.

---

[1]Marion Behr and Wendy Lazar, *Women Working Home* (New Jersey: WWH Press, 1981), p. 11.
[2]Ibid.
[3]Ibid.
[4]Ibid., p. 38.
[5]Ibid., p. 99.
[6]"Selling Romance, British Style," *Time* (December 21, 1981), p. 66.
[7]Susan Muenchow and Jean Biddle, "Working Parents—1981 Style," *Parents' Magazine* (September, 1981), p. 65.

12

Making the Commitment

> The biggest disease today is not leprosy or tuberculosis, but rather the feeling of being unwanted, uncared for and deserted by everybody.
>
> Mother Teresa of Calcutta

BEFORE MY HUSBAND, Don, and I moved to our small lake community, we decided to take a walk on the boardwalk one lovely summer evening. We were just about to purchase a house near the lake and wanted to take one last look at the setting. Halfway down the boardwalk, we were stopped by the policeman on duty who informed us that it was past the curfew hour and the boardwalk was closed. We chatted with this man briefly because we wanted to gain his perspective on the community.

"What's it like here?" I queried.

"It's the guts of hell," the policeman countered.

"What do you mean 'the guts of hell'? Look at all of this natural beauty and the comfortable upper-middle-class homes."

The policeman started to explain his statement. He

pointed out that the boardwalk was the hangout for a segment of the town's young people, summer and winter. The teen-agers, some of whom were as young as thirteen, milled around the boardwalk, drinking and taking drugs. Their parents were never seen around the boardwalk, and some dropped their young teens off, knowing full well how they would spend their time.

This policeman expressed deep concern for these middle-class young people who appear rootless and without inner moorings. He said that on many occasions he had spoken to the youth about the lack of meaning in their lives. "These kids are living in a moral vacuum. I don't know where their parents are or what their parents  are doing, but the kids have all the money they need and little apparent supervision. It's pretty gritty up here in 'divorce acres.'"

Months later, after we had settled into our new home, enrolled one child in the junior high and another in an elementary school, the local newspaper carried a series of articles about the boardwalk and the teen-agers who hang out there. The articles said in effect that the teen-agers had no fear of reprisal from the police or any other adult, for that matter, and they resisted any attempts to disband their groups. Any police intervention was met with jeers, obscenities, and screams. The police felt their hands were tied in trying to deal with the teen-agers, because they simply fell through the cracks in the criminal justice system and were back on the streets without receiving significant punishment or discipline.

According to the newspaper articles, both the police and the shopkeepers on the boardwalk wondered what had happened to parents. Although it was common knowledge that the youth drank and took drugs on the boardwalk, the parents of this community either expected the police to baby-sit or they did not care enough to supervise their children's activities. Emotionally, if not physically, they had simply abdicated their parental responsibilities.

Sadly, this affluent New Jersey town is not unique. If we are to believe what we read, teen-agers are adrift throughout America. Exposed to alcohol, drugs, and sexual experiences, kids are growing up in an atmosphere that leads many to live sad lives.

But during the same hours that teen-agers are milling around the boardwalk and similar areas in America, some mothers and fathers are attempting to counter cultural values and, standing against a hedonistic culture, are rearing beautiful, well-disciplined children, often in difficult circumstances. I would like to introduce you to one such family.

Lynn and Ron had just graduated from high school when they decided to marry without parental approval. Borrowing a car for the occasion, they crossed the North Carolina state line to South Carolina where they were married before an unknown justice of the peace. They married, in part, to flee their families. But they were also in love and had found in each other a confidant and concerned friend.

To compound their difficulties, Lynn soon became pregnant, and their first son was born eleven months after their wedding. Chris was a loved and wanted child. His parents viewed his coming with anticipation, having little understanding of how their lives would change. Ron now became the sole support of his little family. With their old car and the furnishings of their small apartment purchased on credit, this family tried to make it.

Soon, however, their car died because Ron forgot to keep oil in the engine, and within a brief time they were mired in debt, floundering in poverty.

"We were so poor," said Lynn, "that when Chris was a baby and we went to the grocery store to buy food, we would first buy all the baby food that Chris needed, then leave the store and count our money. We bought our food with whatever we had left. For a long time all we ate were bread and potatoes. In the process we both grew obese. When Ron was Santa one year at the plant where he worked, he didn't even have to wear a pillow. The costume just fit." With that Lynn pulled out a photograph of a large, red-suited man whose grin seemed forced.

Their self-images, already poor, plummeted. The low point of those early years of financial struggle came one day when they walked into a department store and saw a former high school friend. "We went up to him to say hello, and he stared at us without recognition. When we told him who we were, he was incredulous. He simply could not believe the transformation that had taken place in a few short years."

When their second child, Michelle, was born, the young parents were deeper in debt. Ron had changed jobs, giving insurance sales an unsuccessful try. Creditors hounded the young couple. When Lynn came home from the hospital, the electric company threatened to cut off their power. It was a cold and bleak February, and each day as some creditor knocked on their door, the couple's anxiety deepened.

Married for six years, poor, Ron became so depressed that he thought his family would be better off without him. At least alone, Lynn would, he felt, find others more helpful. Desperate, Ron decided to commit suicide.

Because they had no garage, he bought a hose to bring his car exhaust inside the automobile. Fortunately, the hose did not fit. In growing despair, Ron finally told Lynn about his suicide attempt, realizing how distressed she would be but feeling that he needed to reach out.

"That was a turning point in our lives," stated Lynn in conversation over coffee. "Before that time Ron and I had believed we could handle our lives and our needs without outside help. Our pride did not allow us to share the truth of our poverty with family members. How often my mother-in-law dropped by to show me her new dress, unaware that our cupboards were literally bare. We simply did not want anyone to know how terrible things were.

"But after Ron's attempt to take his own life, I knew we could not continue as before. Although I had become a Christian in my teens, it was at this point that I gave God control of my life. Ron saw the change in me and began to search for God, letting Him in at the cracks of his life. But God honored this honest searching.

"After this critical occasion in our lives, things started to change, slowly, imperceptibly, at first. Our first project was to climb out of the pit of debt we had allowed ourselves to get into. We stopped using easy credit, made a workable budget, and tightened our already-tight belts. We had felt when we were first married that we, like other young American couples we knew, deserved possessions. Now we saw how this attitude had led us into a kind of bondage, with a mountain of debt as the result of our unwise spending. We learned to be grateful for all that God had given us—each other, our children, our home. Even the smallest items that we were able to purchase gave us pleasure. Those days if we had enough money left over at the end of the week to buy a bag of popcorn, we had a celebration."

During the years when Lynn and Ron were paying off their debts and attempting to restore their credit rating, they could not afford to go out for meals or entertainment. They learned, however, to make the most of their evenings at home. Ron who is an undiscovered comedian, taught his sons, Chris and Brad (the child born three years after Michelle), to improvise routines with him. Lynn and Michelle play straight men to the trio, and the house often rings with laughter.

Once when I was visiting this family and listening to

the humor, I realized that I was laughing much more than usual. I asked Lynn if her family always laughed so often and so heartily.

"We laugh more now than we did during those early, hard years. But even in the deepest poverty there were those evenings when we could forget the harsh reality of our lives and play with each other and the children. The gift of laughter has graced the dark moments of our lives."

Unlike some couples strapped by inadequate finances, Lynn and Ron did not resent the presence of their children and tried not to take their fears and anger out on them. Before they began living as Christians, however, they did have some terrible times of anxiety and depression. When their lives began to improve, Lynn and Ron worried about Chris. How scarred was he from those years of poverty when his parents were often tense and frightened? From conversations with Chris, his parents concluded that either he did not remember the events because he was too young or else God had healed those memories. Chris has emerged from those years of economic hardship strong and capable.

When he was thirteen, Chris was selected as one of North Carolina's gifted children and went to a nearby college for a summer program with college professors. He was student body president of his junior high and continues to be an "A" student. When he was in high school, Chris worked at a restaurant, earning thirty-five dollars a week. With this he funded his used car and gave his family lovely, generous gifts. One Christmas he took Michelle and Bradley shopping and supplemented their meager funds with his own.

Now nineteen and a freshman in college on full scholarship, Chris has never experimented with drugs and he is still a virgin. He has a good self-concept and a close relationship with both his parents. He is also an itinerant youth minister who travels to preach at various Baptist churches on weekends.

Michelle and Bradley are also able students who view the world with open, eager faces. Both are direct, and when asked how they feel about a particular issue, can answer with disarming candor. Openness is valued in the Harrison family.

Committed to their children, Lynn and Ron are also deeply committed to each other. "Even in our worst days we did not contemplate divorce," stated Lynn. "We had no one to run to. Our families would not have taken us in. We knew that we only had each other, at least at first, and this knowledge created solidarity. I did run away once. I packed my suitcase and walked down the road, still within sight of our home. It was late evening so none of the neighbors saw me. I sat down on the suitcase in the middle of the road and stewed. Since I had no where to go, after I calmed down, I simply went back home.

"Adversity kills many marriages. Our poverty—though it was terrible and lasted for eleven years—taught us how to work with each other and create a rock-like marriage. I know our marriage will last, even with the cultural assaults of the eighties. Ron and I have been through so much and we know each other like we know our own bodies. Sometimes I feel so close to my husband that I do not know where his body ends and mine begins. His hand is mine and my arm is his. We really are one."

What about this family's economic state? When they finally pulled out of debt and learned that they had an excellent credit rating, they began to pray that God would give Ron opportunities for economic advancement since for most of the years of their marriage his income has been either the sole or main support for the family. For a number of years he held a middle management position with a large corporation, and this provided sufficient funds for the family.

About a year ago I had a lovely experience with this family. The six of us were attending a funeral together, and at the funeral a young woman who did not know the Harrisons came up to them and said, "It is obvious that you love each other very much." She was struggling with some unhappiness in her own life and was drawn to Lynn's family. After she left, Lynn turned to me and said. "You know, lots of people tell me that Ron and I have beautiful children and that they love each other in a close and unusual way. To me, they seem like usual children with their gripes and hurts and joys. Obviously, because I am their mother they are special to me, but do they really stand out as special to others?"

I assured her that this was so. What I did not say then but recognized later is that Ron and Lynn in their small house are producing children who are works of art—living, breathing products of love, concern, and deep commitment. It is becoming increasingly unusual to see children in harmony with themselves and others, children who love their parents dearly and respect authority.

In an age when children shout abuse at police with impunity and scream at any adult who exercises authority, these children are a tremendous tribute to their parents. Their success in life, their open faces, and their ability to love themselves and others are, in large measure, the result of their parents' ability to make and keep commitments.

Using any sociological yardstick that one wishes, this couple should by all rights be divorced. Married at eighteen, parents within the first year, fugitives from unhappy parental homes, trapped for some eleven years in poverty while at the same time increasing their family size, without the benefit of higher education, both should be on the societal garbage heap. Lynn should be struggling on welfare and Ron should be adrift, trying to find himself. Instead, their marriage is vital and intimate and their children are reasonably whole.

Months ago I revisited this family just to update my knowledge of their lives. I found the whole family alive with joy. Ron had decided to leave his secure middle management position and enroll in a Baptist seminary. He and Chris are both freshmen at schools about forty miles apart.

Ron and Lynn did not arrive at this decision easily or overnight. Over a period of two years Ron felt that God was urging him to go into the ministry and literally turn his back on any financial security. Lynn found this especially difficult since she remembered too well their years of deep poverty.

"God had to prove to us that He would take care of us, and the way He did it was to increase our expenses so that we were always two hundred dollars short each month. Then He came through with what we needed," said Lynn.

"What happened was that God gave me a new job in South Carolina while Lynn remained in North Carolina with the children, waiting to sell the house," added Ron. "Well, the house simply did not sell; in fact, during a six-month period the realtors showed the house only twice. It was during this period, while I was living with a Christian family and we could not meet our expenses, that God taught us a deeper level of trust."

Ron related a dream that he had had during this period away from his family, in which he saw himself standing in front of a Baptist church in a town in Florida. The sign outside the church had his name on it as the minister. "I didn't even know there was a town with that name in Florida," Ron exclaimed, "but I decided to call the First Baptist Church there anyway. I asked the church secretary if she would send me a post card of the church since I had been told the building was attractive. When the card arrived, it was the same church I had seen in my dream!"

Ron and Lynn embraced the idea that God had a better life for them than a middle-class suburban existence. Once hooked on acquisitiveness, they were willing to sell their house so they could use the equity to pay off any outstanding debts. When I saw them, they were literally full of joy as they prepared to live modestly during the years of seminary on what the two of them earned.

As it worked out, Ron and Lynn had to move to the mountain town where they presently live without any employment and with little cash. "We tried to find work before our move," Lynn told me, "but nothing came through. But we didn't feel we could turn back. Ron had already given up his job at the plant, and, besides, we knew in our hearts that God wanted Ron in seminary.

"We were scared as we moved into the rented house on that cold December day. We had only enough money to last until the first of February, and we didn't know where February's rent would come from."

In time Lynn found a job in a department store and Ron found work washing dishes at a local motel several evenings a week. He also located a job cleaning a bowling alley each morning, a job he does at 5:00 A.M. Lynn is home with their children in the mornings, and Ron greets them every afternoon.

One of the other seminary students told Ron that God did not require him to do such menial work, but Ron only laughed in reply. In a town where any work is hard to come by, Ron feels grateful that he has found two part-time jobs which give him some time for school and his family.

In a recent telephone conversation Lynn said that she and Ron have no regrets. They are daily experiencing God's love and care. "We still don't earn enough money for all our needs, but God will encourage someone in our church to bring a load of wood or a large bag of frozen vegetables, or a check will unexpectedly arrive from a friend or relative. Once even Chris's roommate donated twenty dollars for rent. And the February rent? It was paid several days before it was due."

Lynn said that their lives contain times of joy and peace because they know beyond any doubt that they are living in the center of God's will. "This kind of peace is hard to come by, and once you experience it you don't want to lose it, even if you have to confront and go beyond your fears."

She also told me, after she and Ron had a chance to read this chapter, that while the events had occurred in their early marriage just as I had recounted them they do not remember the pain of their poverty. It is as if God has covered those memories, even the memory of Ron's attempted suicide, with a special grace.

"There is," Lynn added," no real poverty for the Christian. Poverty is a state of mind, and it was ours. It is ours no longer."

These people are from the ranks of dedicated, good parents in America today who go unrecognized and unapplauded. Since they are not rich or famous or powerful, their lives win no accolades from the media. Yet how beautiful are lives such as these in an increasingly dark age. And how desperately we need their example.

13

Teaching Our Children How To Live

> Children have changed dramatically in the last ten years. My students no longer are motivated to learn, to do well so that they can go on to college. This apathy depresses me. What *are* parents teaching kids at home?
>
> a junior-high math teacher

DURING THE PAST twenty years, we have witnessed the erosion of traditional values, and we have seen the social institutions that upheld them—namely, the school and the church—beat a steady retreat.

As church and school have grown defensive or strangely silent and as parents have left home for work, young people have grown up in a vacuum. I was not personally sensitive to this until about nine years ago when I held my last full-time teaching position at a high school. At that time I encountered the apathy and emptiness that have become characteristic of so many adolescents today. My favorite class was a group of college-bound eleventh graders in a Connecticut high school who were poor readers and poorer writers. As I drilled them in the basics of grammar, saw to it that they wrote a theme a week (unheard of teacher-torture in the eighties), I discovered that they had little to say.

I queried them about their lives. How did they spend those after-school hours? Middle-class, with parents who gave them whatever they desired, most merely went home at 2:30, snacked, turned on the television, and lay on the sofa, mesmerized, until bedtime. I was appalled.

Did they spend hours each week in meaningful conversations with their parents? Most did not. Many did not especially like their parents and viewed the whole process of communication as a waste of time. What about getting a part-time job? They did not see any real need for this. Did they hold any belief so strongly that it gave their life ultimate meaning? Was I kidding, they wanted to know. They believed in having a good time and "partying." Apart from this hedonism, what else existed?

Sadly, while I held these open exchanges with the students, one bright child of professional parents sat in a stupor. His blood-stained shirt-sleeves bore evidence of his heroin habit that all, including school authorities and parents, seemed to know about but were apparently unable to stop. Though I spoke with the boy and troubled the principal about this wasted life, nothing happened; he continued to sleep through his classes and much of his life.

I began to view this little class with missionary zeal. Not only was I determined to teach them the basics of composition and expose them to great literature, but I determined to expose them to meaning as well. I asked a good friend, a nun and latecomer to religious vows, to come and tell the class why she had given up a career in her late thirties to join an order. In so doing, Sister Dorothy, possessor of joy and a good sense of humor, spoke about finding God and purpose for living. The students were so entranced with her that at the year's end we purchased plants and flowers, drove to the convent, and planted a beautiful token of our regard for Sister Dorothy.

I was so moved by these good-natured but directionless students that much of my mothering has been affected as a consequence. I certainly did not want my daughters, then one and three, to grow up with so much emptiness inside. I determined to teach them my beliefs even though these values might be rejected later. At least when they grew up, they would have something to push against. I started with discipline.

When I spoke with a young mother about writing this book, she, a doctor's wife, said, "Please write about the child's need for discipline. So many of my husband's patients haven't any idea about where to start in disciplining their children."

I was a child who grew up without firm and consistent discipline. When my mother and I had contests of will, I knew that if I persisted long enough I would win. Thus, I grew to adulthood with little respect for authority and with the deep feeling that if she really loved me, mother would have stood firm. Now I see that some parents just simply do not understand the contest and, while loving their children, allow them to grow up with an untamed will. Yet evidence reveals that undisciplined children, at base, feel unloved.

It was not until I was thirty that I understood that life was disciplining me severely. When my marriage ended and I could not persuade my husband to continue the union, I finally encountered the ultimate contest I could not win. I could not cajole, manipulate, or in any way control the situation. How I wished then that I had experienced firm, consistent limits while growing up. Parents discipline with more gentleness than does life.

A child must have discipline from an early age. (One mother said that a child first hears the word *no* when he is nursing at mother's breast, bites her nipple with those new teeth, and she removes the breast with a resounding *no!)* I learned with my daughters that the battles I had lost when they were two were fought again at four and six if the lessons had not been learned. A wise older mother who had raised three fine human beings took me aside when my girls were young and said, "Brenda, if you give your girls the consistent love and discipline they need until the age of six, you will discover that most of your work is done." Marty was right. Most of the battles are fought in the first six years when the child's attitudes are being shaped, and disciplining is much easier after that. Of course, if mothers do not understand this, they are in for rough years later.

A mid-thirties mother told me of a conversation she had had with her neighbors at a coffee klatsch where the other women spoke of being afraid of their adolescent sons who towered over them. These women no longer felt able to discipline their older children for fear the adolescents would assault them physically. Obviously, these were children who had not been disciplined consistently and firmly throughout childhood. If a mother has established herself as a parent in charge, she can continue to set limits for her adolescents even if they are bigger and stronger than she. And she can do so without fear.

One woman who was struggling with her new status as separated mother handled her son's rebellion admirably. The boy, who had been a good student, got in with the wrong crowd and was, at fourteen, beginning to experiment with drugs. His worried mother decided she had only one recourse: She told him that if he did not call his friends and tell them that he could no longer associate with them, he would need to pack his bag and leave home. "I love you too much to helplessly watch you throw away your life," his mother said. Her strategy worked. Within twenty-four hours the boy had called his friends, confronted them honestly, and opted for family life instead.

In an era when child abuse abounds, articles are written decrying any form of physical punishment. These writers believe fiercely that if a parent turns Janice over a knee for a few well-deserved wallops, eventually that same parent will throw Janice against the wall or burn her with cigarettes. Yet if one reads the psychological profile of an abusive parent, one reads about an individual who experienced physical abuse and great emptiness as a child. Discipline does not fall in the same category as child abuse, nor are loving parents who discipline their children child abusers under the skin.

I have known mothers who spanked their children's bottoms with their hands, others who used wooden spoons. Some who shrank from any form of physical punishment chose to isolate Johnny instead. Whatever a mother decides, some effective discipline is essential. If words and isolation do not work, I have found either the hand or, when they grew older, the wooden spoon effective tools for discipline. My children prefer the spanking. According to them, the spoon temporarily stings their bottoms, but it does not wound their self-esteem—and is over sooner.

In addition to disciplining our children, we who are mothers must teach our children about life. Someone has to teach them how to cope with insults from peers and handle academic failure or success. Someone has to teach them to communicate by lovingly talking with them each day. Someone has to be there in the low moments of life to reinforce a positive self-image or in the golden moments to share in the celebration.

And as we spend time with our children, we must have something to teach them. When they ask about sexual morality, lying, and death, what do we say? Do we pull something out of the distant past, some vague dictum our parents taught us? Or do we encourage them to establish a world view that is biblically based and life enhancing?

One of the saddest recent scenes I witnessed was seeing decent parents, a lawyer and his wife, become incensed against the cultural values of drug usage and early sexuality while possessing no value system other than what their parents had taught them. Scared, these parents hope against hope that *their* children will not become involved with drugs or sex and try to insulate them by wealth. The right school, the right upper-middle-class neighborhood, they hope, will render their children invulnerable.

It is hard to stand against cultural values, particularly if one does not have a well-defined set of values. Take the area of sex and our teen-agers. Since the sexual revolution, the culture has espoused the creed of sexual pleasure and has said that it is okay for teen-agers, as well as adults, to have intercourse with any willing partner. Some articles state that we are rearing the first generation of teen-agers who feel obligated to have intercourse. While some writers agree that teen-agers may be physically ready for intercourse, the feeling is that they are not mature enough emotionally to handle the ramifications of a sexual relationship. Yet teen-agers, exposed to explicit sex in "R" movies and the media, feel that everyone else is having intercourse and something is wrong if they are not as well. Sadly, it seems that the rush is on for adolescents to shed their virginity.

And yet the consequences of teen-age sexuality are grim. In an earlier chapter, we noted the increase in illegitimate births among teen-age girls and the reality of multiple abortions. But how many studies have been done on the effects of sexual experiences on a teen-ager's self-esteem?

Numerous women have told me of negative sexual experiences they had as teen-agers. Sometimes sex resulted in an unwanted pregnancy that usually ended in abortion. A number of these women who now are in their thirties are still dealing with guilt associated with their teen-age abortions. And even if they did not get pregnant, they often based their self-concept, not on the development of skills and talents, but on their sexual prowess or lack of same. An interesting thing then happened. Developmentally, something went on hold, and these same women are doing the identity work in their thirties that they failed to do in their teens. Only now are they learning to base their self-images, in part, on their abilities rather than on the way they relate to men sexually.

What is a mother to do who is concerned about the negative impact of sexual experiences on her teen-agers? Is she to allow them to soak up any exposure to sex in the media and hope for the best? Is she to capitulate to cultural pressures because she finds so little support for her values from her peers or the basic societal institutions of church and school?

If we believe that sex is to be a part of a loving marriage, we cannot afford to be silent but must actively teach our children a biblical view of sexuality.

Christianity has much to say about sex, honesty in human relationships, and the seriousness of human actions. If a mother will read the Bible aloud with her children and discuss the biblical concepts of sex, she will lay the groundwork for the time when her children will come under fire. I have read that children handle the sexual pressures of the moment in large measure based on the values they have received at an earlier time. In short, if we teach our children to be chaste and moral when they are very young, they will have something to draw on as teen-agers.

In our family we read the Bible aloud each morning at breakfast and have worked our way through several books in the Old and New Testaments. As we read of a holy God and confess our own sin, something is happening to all of us. We are becoming more conscious of ourselves as moral beings. The children are, before our eyes, forging a more mature value system which should help them deal with sexual pressure. While there are no guarantees in life, and no mother can predict how her children will handle difficult moral decisions, she can give her children no greater aid than the study of Scripture.

In addition to teaching children positive values, alert mothers can act to reduce cultural influences inside their homes by either monitoring television viewing or selling their television sets. It is fruitless to advocate chastity if the whole family laughs through "Dallas." Kids smell the hypocrisy of that. Besides, television is a waste of time and, as studies show, it can turn children into students with a poor attention span and an unrealistic view of life. In addition, television trains students in the art of passivity.

Years ago I noticed that students who watched lots of television were generally poor readers who wrote impoverished, unimaginative papers. Since they were failing to expose their minds to great literature, they had few literary allusions or examples to use to enrich their writing. Their themes were often rehashed media attitudes and values, rendered without careful thought and evaluation. Also, they viewed life as a succession of bland, unexciting days. Since I did not want my children to become apathetic like the students I struggled to teach, I went home one day and sold our television. The girls were then one and three.

Already Holly loved to sit passively in front of the television. I knew that the baby-sitter kept her set on while the children were with her, but I wanted the hours of our day together to count, so I read to them and did not rely on "Sesame Street" to teach them. Moreover, I wanted the children to develop inner resources and learn to entertain themselves, to give free rein to any slumbering gifts.

C. S. Lewis and his brother Warren created Animal Land to fill up some of the hours of their childhood. My sister and I, while less literary, roamed grandaddy's farm, turning loft and field into distant lands. Television, in addition to devouring hours of children's lives, does not force them to create and play. As spectators, hour by hour, children may watch many fine, educational programs and acquire an impressive vocabulary, but what is happening to their imaginative powers as well as their ability to entertain themselves?

Selling that television set has proved to be one of the best decisions of my life. We have now lived without the tube for twelve years. (I realize that we are in the statistical minority, since some 98 percent of all American families have one or more sets.) What have been the benefits of going against the cultural mainstream?

First, my children have always been able to create their own play for hours at a time. When they were younger, they had marathon doll games during which they constructed whole villages. Their entire bedroom floor was often covered with tiny houses, churches, and shops constructed out of old shoe boxes. With boxes and bits of gaily colored cloth, Holly and Kristen concocted ingenious creations. Their longest doll game lasted for eight hours one Christmas Day when they only emerged from their bedroom for bathroom breaks and meals.

Also, both read widely and well. Holly, at fifteen, reads the periodicals that come into our home, including *Time* and *Fortune,* and makes frequent trips to the public library. She is presently working her way through *War and Peace* for the second time and has been reading on the college level for several years. Her favorite book, which she has read three times, is *Les Misérables*. Kristen, our thirteen-year-old who's more gregarious by nature, will leave any book behind for a friend; nevertheless, she, like her older sister, scores extremely well on any achievement test, particularly in the areas of vocabulary and reading comprehension and is in the gifted program at her school.

Some of our happiest hours have been spent reading aloud as a family each night before bedtime. Starting when Holly was a year old with the illustrated *Mother Goose,* we have tried to read aloud for at least a half hour on most days. I have acquired some knowledge of excellent children's books and have tried to keep well ahead of the girls' development mentally to stimulate their reading interests.

Don and I share the privilege of being reader, while occasionally the children will take a turn. Three years ago we immersed ourselves in *Uncle Tom's Cabin.* We became interested in Stowe after reading a biography and learning that the vision of Tom's death came to her, intact, while she sat in church one morning.

On the night we approached Tom's death, the suspense grew, and we read for more than two hours. We read until young master George buried Tom, at which point the chapter ended and both children convulsed with sobs. When they stopped crying, Don and I spoke quietly about the real presence of evil in the world, but we also mentioned its opposite, exhibited in the sometimes unreal characterization of Tom. We discussed death and the fact that for the Christian, death can be a welcome event, particularly when life is too painful.

Good fiction has the power to mold and change lives. When we read *Heidi* aloud, scarcely an eye was dry, and during the winter of our financial struggle we warmed ourselves by the fire of *Little Women.* Of late we have read Dickens' *David Copperfield,* Charles and Mary Lamb's *Tales from Shakespeare,* and Gunther's *Death Be Not Proud.*

For a mother interested in the character development of her children, few investments reap greater reward than hours spent reading aloud. I can watch the girls' thinking change as they encounter ideas in the classics. They grow more sensitive to the underdog, to choices between good and evil. And while television occasionally delivers a fine or touching program, it is no substitute for the experience of sitting on a sofa, touching, while mother or father reads aloud what the best minds have written.

What we discover when we read great literature is that many of the great writers were Christians. Lewis says in *Mere Christianity*, "Nearly all the greatest love poetry in the world has been produced by Christians." And Lewis's own Narnia stories can never be fully understood apart from his Christian faith.

In addition to the positive effect of family reading upon the children, I have tried to expose the girls to other women who can serve as effective models for them. To counteract the models the culture holds up—Farrah, Cheryl, and Brooke—I have looked for women who are loving, who possess a good self-image, and who have a faith in God.

One of these women is Susie, mother of three small children and wife of Will, a doctor. The oldest of seven children, Susie grew up on a large farm in Asheville, North Carolina, with loving and accomplished parents.

After graduation from Wellesley, Susie spent some months in graduate school and then toured Europe, backpacking, as did many of her generation. Eventually, she wound up at Swiss L'Abri where she became a Christian. In time Susie joined the L'Abri staff as a worker, first in Switzerland and later in England, where I first met her.

Soon after I arrived with most of my worldly goods (three pieces of stuffed luggage and three boxes of toys) at Ealing L'Abri, Susie came over to my apartment to help me get settled. She was one of the first members of the community to extend herself to the three of us. Susie took a real interest in Holly and Kristen. She taught them how to swim, spent time baking with them in her kitchen, and taught them Bible stories on Sunday mornings. In so doing, Susie rounded out the parenting I was struggling to give the girls.

Later Susie married Will, an English doctor, and somehow, eventually, we all ended up in Asheville where we picked up the threads of a rich and lasting friendship. Once again Susie became involved in the lives of my children.

Now living near the farm where she grew up, Susie, who has three children of her own, gave the girls horseback riding lessons, took them bathing nude in the algae-covered horse trough, and taught them about gardening as they helped her weed. Even though the girls grumbled about the latter, they enjoyed the swimming and the square dancing in the meadow enough to tolerate the weeding. Though we now live in New Jersey, we still visit Susie yearly. This next week Holly and Kristen will spend several happy days with Susie and her family.

I who spent five years as a single parent needing help with my children am immensely gratified by Susie's interest in Holly and Kristen. If I searched for a long time, I could not find another young woman who would be a better role model for my daughters. Not only is she compassionate and friendly, but I trust Susie's world view. As a Christian she shares the value system Don and I espouse and she lives it in her own inimitable style. She and Will have not only taken many teen-agers into their home for a period of time, but they opened their home last year to a young woman who chose to carry her illegitimate baby to term. While Susie parented this young woman, Will was her physician—and all their help was freely given.

Children and values. We cannot neglect the teaching of values if we have any desire to counter the cultural emphasis on sex, violence, power and money. Our children do grow up, and they must find something to live by. If we fail to provide life-enhancing values for them, they will look to their peers, their culture, their own devices, in which case they stand to lose.

I shall long remember the adolescent girl who sat on my sofa one summer night, weeping. Her parents had just discovered that she had a sexual relationship with a young man and, too late, informed her that they had hoped she would remain a virgin until marriage. "Why didn't they tell me?" my young friend wailed. "Why did they fail to teach me their sexual values?" And she wept because she had grown up in a vacuum, testing and creating her own ethical system which was sometimes flimsy at best.

We *must* actively seek to counter cultural pressures in our children's lives. They are worth it and they need it. But as we struggle to do so, we will realize that the isolated nuclear family is a lonely entity. We need others, not only to round out our children's lives, but also to provide us with vital human fellowship.

14

We Can't Do It Alone

> Let him who cannot be alone beware of community. . . . Let him who is not in community beware of being alone.
>
> Dietrich Bonhoffer

AN ARTICLE IN the *New York Times* stated that while mothers of illegitimate children who started child bearing when they were seventeen years old or younger had more social and academic problems than peers, they were better parents if they had support from either their mothers or grandmothers. Otherwise, they and their children suffered from what the writer termed "mother aloneness." The children did not suffer just because mother was unmarried, but because mother was totally alone, without any help for herself or her child.[1]

"Mother aloneness"—what a poignant phrase. I remember those periods of "mother aloneness" in my first marriage when my young husband drove to work each day and left me thirty miles behind in suburbia with two babies. Those were some of the worst days of my life.

Then when our marriage ended, I experienced "mother aloneness" in spades.

It was that "mother aloneness" that drove me to England, seeking Christian community. From that experience I learned that all of us need "community," or as Dietrich Bonhoffer calls it, "life together," whether we are married or single, young or old. To illustrate the richness of "life together," I would like to use as examples two different communities: L'Abri Fellowship and the Bruderhof or the Hutterian Society of Brothers as it is also called.

L'Abri was founded by Edith and Francis Schaeffer in Huémoz, Switzerland, more than twenty-five years ago. Francis Schaeffer, who had been a midwestern minister, and his wife Edith believed that God was calling them to go to Switzerland for a work that He would give them and which He would support without advertisement. This family, believing in the authenticity of this call, eventually settled in Huémoz and opened their home to all who came. As a result of their faith, L'Abri Fellowships exist in several European countries and another opened last year near Boston. It was after reading the book *L'Abri* by Edith Schaeffer that I moved my small family to England, where Schaeffer told me Christians were buying and renting flats and houses close to the Ealing L'Abri in order to experience some form of a shared life.

What did I find at L'Abri? I found thinking adults who believed in biblical truth and this fact colored their whole approach to life and each other. Moreover, many had come there not only to learn deeper spiritual truths, but also to follow the Holy Spirit's leading into a life of deeper sharing. This meant, practically speaking, that they were willing to work on difficult relationships and commit to speaking the truth lovingly to each other. It meant they were willing to seek and grant forgiveness.

I who had all the wounds and needs that other separated women possess found what my life so desperately needed—people who cared deeply. As I grew to know and love many of these Christians, I discovered that, unlike earlier periods of my life, I did not have to be employed to enjoy the companionship of adults. Katie, Barney, Susie, Will, John, Penny, Dick, Mardi, and Ros as well as many others, became friends who have profoundly influenced my life. I now had the essential support system my life lacked as a woman alone in suburbia.

These friends helped in the discipline of my children. They invited us for meals, and shared holidays. And over the course of two years, they gave so much love and acceptance that my feelings of self-worth were greatly enhanced. No longer did I possess a lonely life, vulnerable to empty, exploitive relationships. In these loving friendships, I felt in some real sense that I had finally come home.

My life has never been the same. Internalizing so much love and strength which came from shared values, I became addicted to a life of deeper sharing, and wherever I have lived since have tried to find some form of Christian community, sometimes without success. That experience is a flame that, however dim it grows, refuses to be extinguished.

Moreover, not a few of these Christians are still in my life. We are scattered now in Scotland, London, North Carolina, New Jersey, and Seattle, yet we keep the friendships viable and see each other periodically. It is enormously comforting to me that the friends God gave at that painful period of my life are yet in my life, providing continuity.

I shall always be grateful to the Schaeffers and L'Abri. Because of their faith and willingness to trust God, a work was begun in Switzerland that eventuated in the little Christian community which congregated in Ealing. And when my life upended, a place of healing existed for me and my children.

During the year before I moved to England, I was casting about for an alternative lifestyle and I discovered the communal life of the Bruderhof in northwestern Connecticut. Founded in Sannerz, Germany, by Eberhard and Emmy Arnold, this community gathered together in 1920 to live "a life of simple sharing."

> People came from all spheres of life to this little group. After a time in intense searching, testing, and growth, a small nucleus remained, who felt called to show that under the rulership of God men could live a life of loving harmony and brotherhood.[2]

Persecution by the Nazis led the members of the Bruderhof to move first to Liechtenstein in 1934 and later to England in 1937. Although their community life expanded in England, the pressures of World War II caused the Bruderhof to emigrate to Paraguay. During their twenty years in South America, the Bruderhof found that most of their "seeking guests" came from America, so they eventually moved again, this time to the United States. They now have three communities, totaling over 1,000 people, and support themselves by making the successful line of children's toys called Community Playthings.[3]

The life of the Bruderhof is based on Jesus' Sermon on the Mount and the pattern of the shared life found in Acts 4. All things are held in common, which means that no one becomes a member of the Bruderhof without giving his possessions to the community. Realizing that men and women are sinful, the members state that each day lived in community is a gift from the Holy Spirit. The family forms the core unit of the community, and the people live in simple, spartan apartments, the size of which depends exclusively on family size.

What impressed me deeply, feeling as devastated as I did at that time, was their joy. I witnessed it on the open faces of their children who, unlike many other American children, still retained their innocence. Regarded by all members as gifts from God to be nurtured and guided, Bruderhof children are treated with kindness and courtesy. I heard their joy in the English and German songs they sang when they gathered in the communal dining room for meals. This hovering, palpable joy touched my deep loneliness and grief, awakening a longing to some day experience that same joy when my suffering ceased.

Working separately—the men in the factory making the sturdy wooden toys or in the print shop publishing a catalog and books; the women teaching in the school, cleaning, cooking or dressing dolls that are later sold—both parents are home with all but the smallest children after the communal midday meal until 2:00 P.M. (The tiniest children are napping at the baby house.) From 2:00 to 3:00 P.M. mothers are home with all their children. Then it is back to work for several hours.

Bruderhof fathers do not, as many of their American counterparts, lose touch with their young children due to work pressures. Unlike many American fathers who commute to work and still put in sixty hours a week, Bruderhof fathers are close at hand and share three meals each day with their families. Nor are Bruderhof mothers pining away because of loneliness and boredom. On the whole, life in Bruderhof contains much that is missing in American society. When I asked various members about their life together, all spoke of being happier in community and most said they did not see how we Americans could continue to function as isolated, nuclear families.

The years in London and the visits to the Bruderhof have led me to ask why young mothers who choose to stay home with their children need to experience lonely, empty days. Obviously, few can or will uproot their lives to join a Christian community and thus escape isolation. But one does not have to travel far to find other mothers experiencing some of the same problems and concerns. Why can't mothers band together in small groups for some semblance of a shared life? At the very least, these support groups could provide emotional support, shared insights about marriage and child care, or the trading of skills. These small groups could also enable women with like values to stand against cultural pressures as they live the lives they desire.

About a year ago I gave an all-day seminar on the current pressures women in America experience, at which I shared major ideas from this book. The response was overwhelmingly positive. Women thanked me for articulating some of their concerns and asked how they could start support groups.

Although no authority on groups or group dynamics, I have led workshops for divorced mothers and, with my husband Don, have worked for many months with a singles group. Basically, we learned what we could about group dynamics, chose a format for the group meeting, located a place for the adults and another place nearby for the children, found someone to work with the children, and advertised in the local newspaper.

Don and I learned several important things from this experience. First, content is strategic; without it, any group can degenerate into a gripe session. The mind needs something substantial to grind on, and group discussion flows best out of the brief presentation of a topic that vitally interests the people present.

Second, the group needs to include in-depth sharing usually fostered by the group leader. Women like to share deeply—*long* to share deeply—but are often afraid. They need permission that filters down from the top as the leader risks self-exposure. Without the leader's exposure of personal pain and struggle, the group members will seldom open up, and eventually people will cease to come.

I was recently part of a Christian group whose leader fought in-depth sharing, stating that all were present to do a "job for Jesus" and not to get their interpersonal needs met. Not surprisingly, many of the women dropped out of the organization because they hated the resultant superficiality.

As human beings, we need support. We wither in moral or spiritual isolation. To achieve our human potential and to realize our gifts, we must interact with others. But to say that we must go to the marketplace to find adult interaction is to consign our children to loneliness and to be extremely limited in looking for answers.

As one looks at societal institutions, it is obvious that the organized church provides the natural vehicle for meeting human needs. Thousands of church buildings which go unoccupied during most of the week could be utilized for support groups, counseling centers, teaching seminars—to name a few. Too often church buildings are locked due to the threat of vandalism. And yet the church could be a *place* of healing, a societal hospital, if the buildings were open and if Christians were inside, available to help.

During the years I have talked to divorced men and women, I have heard a steady refrain; it is, *we have nowhere to go*. Living in a society that encourages divorce, these men and women find that this same society provides no help for those going through the experience. And the divorced are only one segment of our society currently in need.

L'Abri and the Bruderhof show us that it is possible for us to reach out to each other—with the Holy Spirit's help. As Christians, we must not cut ourselves off from each other, insulated by fear, pride, and material comfort.

It will not always be easy. The telephone will ring at

inopportune moments; someone in need will reach out when we do not feel like responding. Someone will drop by for coffee when we do not wish to talk. But if we do respond to the person in front of us with something of Christ's love, we will discover that we no longer feel so alone or half alive.

And we are on our way to finding that hovering, palpable joy that graces the shared life.

---

[1]"Mother Aloneness," *New York Times* (February 4, 1979), p. 20f.

[2]Information comes from a pamphlet called "The Bruderhof—a Christian Community," which may be obtained from any one of the three communities.

[3]The three Bruderhof communities are located in Norfolk, Connecticut; Rifton, New York; Farmington, Pennsylvania.

15

Unhooking Mother's Guilt

> I am sixty years old and, because of the way my children have turned out, I feel like a failure as a mother.
>
> —a discouraged mother

MOTHERS, IT WOULD seem, are exquisitely vulnerable to guilt. More than fathers, they carry the burden of their children's psychological well-being, and a large part of their self-esteem is based on the way their children turn out. No matter how mother lives her life, whether she works during the years her children are growing up or stays home, she is open to feelings of guilt if her children mess up their lives.

This summer I accompanied my husband to Washington, D.C., on a business trip and spent several days in the Library of Congress reading books on working mothers. While volume after volume advocated career for mother, nearly all said she suffered from a painful malady: guilt.

A physician-mother describes that guilt well.

> For years I have struggled with the guilt of leaving my children to do my work. I have told myself that it can be done—indeed I need to do it and I make a contribution. And yet, I'm torn. I'm two people. My identity constantly undergoes daily dramatic changes. The worst of it is that I feel like I'm doing a lousy job both at home and in my medical practice. I don't think this conflict will be resolved until the children are grown. Already I have regrets about not spending enough time with them, and I know that once they are grown and gone I'll live with the guilt and regret for the rest of my life. I am a doctor. I can't not be. I am also a mother. I can't not be that either.[1]

I spoke with a young single woman who works in a Washington, D.C., office with bright, ambitious young mothers who unload their guilt each morning. Jean recounted the ritual these mothers go through as they share their concern about sick children at home alone or babies in day-care. "It is," said Jean, "as if they attempt to off-load their guilt by sharing it with each other."

An article by Naomi Munson entitled "Having Babies Again" addresses mother-guilt. Munson writes about the young ambitious women in her Manhattan office who are now "into pregnancy." Having tried "cocaine and caviar, shot the rapids in a canoe, done the Carribean and Aegean, kept clean with Gene and dressed for success, tried the new sexuality and the new celibacy," these women feel that babies will fill the void in their lives.

So they have their amniocentesis, attend their natural childbirth classes with husbands in tow, and become mothers. Then it's off to day-care for baby and back to the office for mother. For as Munson writes:

> . . . while *having* babies is very much the thing, taking the time and expending the energy to raise

> them properly is still definitely déclassé. These babies are conceived, paradoxically enough, with no thought for the future.[2]

Conception is simply the next step in mother's search for fulfillment.

Yet these mothers, according to Munson, are experiencing a new emotion—guilt. While they trot out all the arguments for the working mother—that it's healthy for a young child to be separated from mother, that it's quality and not quantity time that counts, that an unhappy mother is not fit company for her child—they still feel guilty. "The struggle here is clearly internal. It is themselves they seek to convince of the purity of their motives, the righteousness of their actions, while all their instincts tell them that they are doing something wrong."[3] With humor, Munson states that babies don't care about mother's search for fulfillment; they simply want her home with them.

I have just finished reading Jessie Bernard's *Self-Portrait of a Family* and think it is safe to say that this internationally known authority on the family, winner of numerous accolades in the field of sociology, suffered from extreme guilt as a mother.

Becoming a mother for the first time when she was thirty-eight and had already received her doctorate, Jessie welcomed her daughter Dorothy Lee and later her son Claude to an ailing marriage. Earlier she had separated from her husband, a well-known sociologist, and only returned to the marriage to have children. Says Bernard, "I made my return to the marriage contingent on having children."[4]

While Jessie and her husband wanted to have their first two children, David, her last child, was conceived while his father was dying of cancer. Both parents wanted to abort him. Later Jessie learns that for David as a teenager suicide was a "recurring theme" and that even at the age of three he remembered wanting to jump out of a window.

Bernard's book is basically a compilation of letters she exchanged with her children as she traveled around the world, building a career, at the same time she was struggling to rear them as a single parent. Some mothers reading her book will cringe when they learn that she left a three-year-old and six-year-old under the care of her older daughter while she went off to attend a sociology conference.

> Dorothy Lee was barely twelve when I left her in Ostende in charge of the boys while I was off to Liege to give a paper at the meeting of the International Sociological Association. When I told my European and British colleagues at the conference that I had left my three children, the oldest only twelve, alone for a week, they were aghast.[5]

Bernard later felt guilty for doing this, but she told herself and her children that she "could not afford to have children who could not look after themselves."[6]

Bernard tells the reader that she was often out of the country at important moments in her children's lives. Sometimes she missed a child's first day of camp or school. On other occasions she was unable to greet the child who had just arrived home from college or even be at home during a school vacation. Once Bernard had her children move themselves from one state to another in her absence. Putting Dorothy Lee in charge, Bernard left the children meticulous directions in one of her letters.

By her own admission, Bernard was a "peripetatic mother" in flight from her children. The sociologist who wrote in *The Future of Motherhood* that our society cannot afford housewives feels that she neglected her children and occasionally bought them off with money. Although she feels "plenty guilty" about this, Bernard consoles herself by stating that she had "wonderful enough children" who could somehow get by with less mothering than even she seemed to feel they needed.

When she writes to David, the child who seemingly caused her the most worry, the book rings with pathos: "I remember how heartstricken I was to see the joy in your face—you were about three—when I returned from a trip."[7] And later she writes that she knows David did not feel loved.

> I suppose about this time you had given up on ever getting love from me so, in effect, you began to say—in acts, not words—OK, if you won't love me I won't let you love me and began the rejection of me. I suppose your refusal to go away to prep school was a sort of blind clutching to the hope that if you stayed home you could win my love.[8]

Why was Bernard in flight from her children who seemingly had few other adults involved in their lives? She says that she was afraid of becoming a "devouring mother" who looked to her children to meet her emotional needs. In her attempt to avoid making her children her "entire life," Bernard admits that she moved too far in the opposite direction. While she writes that she loves her children, she wonders in a letter to David if "words can make up for years of deprivation."[9]

One cannot read *Self-Portrait of a Family* without thinking in terms of irony. Here is an authority who has spent more than forty years working in the area of the family, who extols professional women—of whom she is one—for their ability to combine career and motherhood, who makes housewives hang their heads in shame and feel they must be wasting their lives. And yet this sociologist writes: "I used to laugh at myself saying that I deserted my own family to talk to other people about families."[10]

And in her seventies when she is surrounded by awards and accolades this woman looks back and ponders her relationship with her children. Her book is an apologia, and one of its chief functions is the exoneration of Bernard's performance as a mother.

While one can admire Bernard's honest portrayal of herself as a fallible mother, it is well to remember that this is the same woman who wrote, "Being a housewife makes women sick." And while Bernard writes convincingly of the isolation and loneliness that plague the stay-at-home mother, the fact that she has also written of neglecting her own children puts her disparagement of the mother who stays home in a different light. While Bernard may well have escaped the pitfalls that befall the American housewife by having an engrossing career, how did her children feel about the loneliness their in-flight mother must have created for them? Bernard is lucky. Whatever her children felt growing up, they worked hard in their letters to set their mother free from her obvious guilt.

Why do working mothers feel guilty? Some writers believe guilt comes from society's attitude toward working mothers. And yet, as stated earlier in the book, it is not the working mother who now has society's disapproval. It is the mother who stays home. Mother now has nearly everyone's permission to work, but apparently permission is not enough.

Munson's explanation of this guilt is closer to the mark.

> . . . these mothers know full well that the defenseless creatures they have borne need not a friendly shove out of the house but a safe haven from what seems to them a chaotic and unmanageable world. They know, too, that only they can provide that haven.[11]

Their guilt, Munson concludes, is "the tribute emotion pays to their failure" to rationalize their absence from their children's lives.[12] Unfortunately, for most of us rationalization is not effective in dealing with something as powerful as guilt. What finally removes our guilt?

The Bible clearly states that guilt abates when we admit that we have fallen short of God's purpose for our lives and ask for His forgiveness. First John 1:9 reads: "If we confess our sins, he is faithful and just and will forgive us our sins and purify us from all unrighteousness" (NIV).

Any mother, whether she works or stays home, can get free of her guilt if she comes to the Father and lives henceforth according to His design for her life. This design will include the mothering of her children in a way that lets her feel good about herself and her mothering.

But, one might counter, is it a sin to leave one's child for long hours to pursue self-fulfillment in a career? Surely, there is nothing to confess. If one feels guilty, however, *something* is creating that sense of guilt. If not society, what? Is it mother's own heart that accuses her, telling her what she knows to be true—that her children need more of her mother-presence? For if mother feels she is giving her children what they need, no one can make her feel guilty.

In addition to the guilt mothers experience when they know they are not giving their children what they need, there is the guilt a mother feels if her children turn out badly. A mother carries this guilt as a stone upon her heart.

Numerous women have come into my life in recent years who feel like failures as mothers because their children are, as adults, lost in successive sexual relationships, divorce, or alcohol. Unable to keep jobs for any length of time, drifting, these children are products of the sixties and seventies. They are not responsible, sexually moral, or ambitious like their Christian parents.

When I spoke to a group of middle-aged women about the ideas in this book, I was struck by the guilt many of them felt. These mothers, who had been there emotionally and physically for their children, felt it was their fault that their children were mucking up their lives. "Where did I go wrong?" wailed one mid-fifties mother who had devoted half her life to the raising of her children.

Is a mother a failure if her children turn out badly? If that mother was sexually promiscuous, an alcoholic, or irresponsible we might be quick to say yes. But what if that mother tried to do her best and invested time and love in her children's lives? If those children live in self-destructive ways or violate her value system, do we call her supermom and condemn her, leading her to believe that her children would have fared better if she had worked during the years they were at home? Or if the child has a working mother, as did a boy in our community, and commits suicide, what then?

The liberating message of the Bible is that no matter what our responsibility for the past, God does not condemn us. As it says in Romans 8:1, "No condemnation now hangs over the head of those who are 'in' Jesus Christ. For the new spiritual principle of life 'in' Christ lifts me out of the old vicious circle of sin and death" (PHILLIPS).

During the writing of this book, I remembered something that generated feelings of guilt in my own life. I had long felt guilty about the quality of mothering Kristen received during the early months of her life. Her father's affair surfaced when she was seven months, and from then on I was consumed with anxiety. Later when she was little more than a year, Thomas left our home and I remained as sole live-in parent. I was deeply depressed for the months before he left and for some months thereafter. Symptomatic of my depression, I experienced weight loss, insomnia, and feelings of helplessness and gloom.

Obviously, my mothering was affected by my depression. I can remember clearly that sometimes during the early months after the revelation of Thomas's affair I nursed my baby and forgot that she lay in my arms. My milk dried up and I switched Kristen to the bottle. But I was not in touch with my baby's signals as I had been with her sister's because I was grieving for the loss of love.

During later years, whenever I thought about Kristen's infancy, I felt guilty. The guilt made it difficult for me to discipline Kristen during the early years of her life. It wasn't until I was in counseling that I accepted the fact that I couldn't change the past, but I could deal with the present. From that day on I became a more effective disciplinarian.

But the wound had not healed. I still believed that Kristen had been denied her birthright—a happy union between parents who loved each other. And over the years I diligently prayed that God would heal my child and make up for that loss.

One day as I wrote about Kristen's birth—her early arrival in the breech position and the pain that attended her delivery as I labored across from an estranged husband who, as I learned later, was in love with someone else—I was overcome with feelings of sadness. I finished the chapter and then lay on the floor, heavy with regret. As I lay there, I prayed and asked God to deal with this part of my past. As if in answer to that petition, my mind began to remember the evidence of His care in the months after Thomas left. Granted, I had been a depressed mother, but God in loving foresight sent the girls a warm surrogate mother for that first year alone. And later when I was ready, He took us to a place where my maternal cup could be filled. So He and I had no problem. But what about Kristen? Did she feel cheated because of the events surrounding her birth, events I had never tried to hide?

Entering Kristen's room that night to kiss her and tuck her in, I lay down beside her for some conversation. Bedtime is one of Kristen's favorite times for those heart to heart conversations. I told her that I had been remembering the circumstances surrounding her birth and wondered how she viewed them. I guess I expected my child to have some of the same feelings of regret and sadness that I felt.

I shall never forget what she said. Reaching out to put her arms around me and snuggle close, Kristen gave me a gift. "Mommy," she said matter-of-factly, "I know you and daddy had a bad marriage when I was born and that you were sad for a long time after he left. I suppose I missed out on things as a baby then. But we are happy now. You and dad love each other and you love Holly and me. That's enough."

As I held my daughter close, my heart agreed. We are a happy family now. God is a giver of second chances. Although I failed to give Kristen the quality of mothering she needed then, God had intervened in our lives and given so much help. Moreover, He started a process of inner healing in my life and the lives of my children that continues today. When I realized this and perceived just how Kristen viewed her life, something inside eased and I have never felt guilty about Kristen's early life since.

God then is ready to liberate us from guilt at any moment in time. Sometimes, however, we are unwilling to forgive ourselves and need to be encouraged to let go of the harsh judgments we hang over our heads. Also, we need to understand that no matter how effective we are as mothers, we can never guarantee that our children will live productive lives or be happy. No matter how much time, love, and care we give our children, they are free agents and are subject to the values and pressures of the age.

Sometimes the very thing that our children need is

for us to step aside and watch God work in their lives, creating the essential changes. Jay's story illustrates this truth beautifully.

One night Jay's parents, Thelma and Bob, came to dinner, and during the hours of conversation that followed coffee, they told an intriguing story of their son's changed life. Apparently, Jay had begun using drugs when he was only eleven years old.

"Jay started innocently enough with marijuana," said Thelma, "but after awhile, he popped any pill he could get his hands on. He took thyroid tablets, pills for heart patients, uppers and downers. It's a miracle that Jay still has a mind and healthy body after all the drugs he took."

Then followed six harrowing years during which Jay ran away repeatedly, when he wandered down the halls at school oblivious to his surroundings, when he slept in the woods at night and the rain did not awaken him, when his worried parents roamed the countryside in the dead of night vainly trying to find him.

"During that time," said Thelma, "I prayed for Jay's safety because I did not know when or if he would overdose." Jay threatened suicide on occasion and once threatened to kill his sister. "That was the night we slept downstairs between their rooms just to protect Robin. The worst part occurred when Jay began to deal drugs, and I knew he was hurting other kids as well as himself. That was hell."

"The day finally came," added Bob, "when I couldn't take any more. I had been a traditional Christian; you know, the kind who goes to church and even teaches Sunday school but who does not really know or believe the Bible.

"Well, one day when I was driving home from work, I spoke to the Lord in a new, familiar way. I told Him that I released Jay into His hands and that He had my permission to do whatever He wanted to do with Jay's life. Thel had released Jay earlier and had gotten rid of her guilt, feeling that Jay was responsible before God for his behavior. But it took me longer to let go.

"Within *eight* days [and Bob began to get excited here], God acted in Jay's life in a dramatic way. It happened this way. Jay had gone to youth group one Sunday night, and as he was walking through the church, he saw money—about five hundred dollars—lying in an open safe in the pastor's office. Jay and a friend took the money, drove off, and the next day started to buy large quantities of drugs. The church discovered both the theft and Jay's new wealth. The elders met and gave Jay an ultimatum: either he would go to Teen Challenge for help or they would call the police. Since Jay had already had trouble with the police, he didn't want to deal with them again.

"So Jay went instead to Teen Challenge, the facility run by Don Wilkerson, which stresses the fact that only Jesus and the help of the Holy Spirit can help drug users construct new lives.

"Within a few months, a dramatic change had occurred in Jay's life. He had become a believer and had been baptized in the Spirit. It was wonderful," said Bob, "to see the change in our son. For one thing, he began talking to us. On an early visit Jay, who had answered us for years in monosyllables, talked for *three* hours."

Jay remained at Teen Challenge for fourteen months, passed his high school equivalency exam, then went to North Carolina where he worked with PTL for a year. Now Jay, who is a handsome blond with a radiant face, works in Sussex county, New Jersey, where he grew up, with teen-agers who are on drugs. Working for an independent organization called The Way Home, Jay and his partner go into the high schools, tell their stories, talk with the kids there and on the streets, and run a coffeehouse ministry on Friday nights.

As one looks at Jay today, it is difficult to believe that

for almost seven years he was lost to life. With his overflowing joy in Christ, it is hard to imagine him as a drug user and dealer.

What brought about this amazing change in a boy who did not respond to his parents' attempts to improve his life? The power of the God of the universe at work in Jay's human life. Not that his parents' love and care were unimportant. Thelma capped this moving story by saying that Jay had come to them after he had changed and thanked them for their influence in his life.

"Jay told us that he was so grateful that we never stopped loving him or hoping that his life would dramatically improve," said Thelma. "How can a Christian ever cease to hope that God will rescue her child and give him a fresh, new life? Not only has Jay found a ministry, but our faith in God has deepened. And God has even removed any pain from the memories Bob and I have of those seven wretched years."

I telephoned Thelma recently at her store, Thelma's Place, where she sells current fashions and dispenses encouragement and joy to her customers. Her voice bubbling happily, Thelma told me of Jay's growing ministry with teen-agers and of the growing outreach she and Bob have with the parents of children involved with drugs. Their message to these beleaguered parents is that God can forgive us and give a new beginning, He can do marvelous deeds in the lives of our children, and He can unhook anyone, parent or child, from guilt.

---

[1]Shirley L. Radl, *How to Be a Mother—and a Person, Too* (New York: Rawson, Wade Pubs., 1979), p. 139.
[2]Naomi Munson, "Having Babies Again," *Commentary* (April, 1981), p. 61.
[3]Ibid., pp. 60–63.
[4]*Self-Portrait of a Family: Letters by Jessie, Dorothy Lee, Claude and David Bernard* (Boston: Beacon Press, 1978), xxi.
[5]Ibid., p. 9.

[6]Ibid.
[7]Ibid., p. 251.
[8]Ibid.
[9]Ibid.
[10]Ibid.
[11]Munson, "Having Babies," p. 62.
[12]Ibid.

16

Finding That Elusive Fulfillment

The one principle of hell is—"I am my own."
George MacDonald

THROUGHOUT THIS BOOK I have urged women to stand against the present cultural view of mothering and to reexamine the place mothers have in their children's lives. I have indicated through the data and the personal accounts that when mothers are either unwilling or unable to be effective parents, their children suffer and carry these wounds into adult life. On the positive side, I have stated that if a mother has the right priorities and places her children's humanity before career success she may find she has experienced the best of both worlds. She will have given her children some essential hours when they needed them; and then when the children are off to school, mother will find she has hours each day to pursue an education, a part-time career, or an avocation.

Women who live this way find that many of the good

feelings they and other women sought "out there" in the world of work—away from home, husband, and children—are available "in here"—at home and with one's family. And when we choose to do what we know in our hearts is best, ignoring the siren's call, even if we suffer economically, we can experience tremendous feelings of self-worth and inner strength.

But I would never advocate that a woman live only for her husband and children. Feminists are correct when they say that this is dead end. But neither can a woman live simply for herself. While this is the modern cultural answer to the question of life's meaning, it too is dead end. To urge women to cease all sacrificial gestures and practice selfishness is to urge them to live truncated lives which produce only ruin and decay. It is also to encourage women to hurt others.

Just last night I spoke to a handsome, sad-eyed young man who is divorced from a wife who left him with their babies while she went off with another man in pursuit of self. This young man is one of a large number who are victims of the modern "virtue" of selfishness.

If we cannot live for our families or for ourselves, what can we live for? We must live for something. Who has not at some point in life cried out, "There must be more to life than this"? Who has not voiced this cry in the quiet of early morning or in the despair of midnight or just after sex or when the momentary joy of success has palled. Only human, we want *more*—more joy, more sex, more money, more love. We are, after all, creatures created for more; but all too often we spend our lives and our energies in a futile search in the wrong direction.

The "more" that we all seek can be found, but it will never be found in things, acclaim, or other people. It must be found in Jesus. I remember the day I found what my life so desperately needed. As I wrote in my first book, *Beyond Divorce,* this moment occurred in my mother-in-law's bedroom just days after my first husband had said that he wanted to leave our marriage. Around me, in broken pieces, lay the stuff of my life. I was about to lose my identity as wife, my husband to another woman, and the father of my children. I was crushed.

"Oh, God!" I cried. "Can you mend my shattered life?" While I did not understand the ramifications of this question or my decision to give Him the controls of my life, I simply knew I could no longer live in the twilight realm I inhabited. Slowly, and often with pain, the God I met first as a teen-ager and ignored during my twenties has taken charge of my life and given a life worth living.

God has surrounded me with Christian love in many forms and provided a second chance to find marital joy. In addition, He cares about my greater wholeness. I had no idea when I wrote the first draft of this book that I would relive some painful parts of my childhood and plunge, temporarily, into depression. Nor did I know that it was possible to get unhooked from the sorrow and guilt surrounding Kristen's birth. But God knew. He also knew just how much my self-image was based on accomplishment and that this area of my psyche needed healing.

During the months of writing and revising this book, of examining my own mothering and the kind of mothering I give my children, I have found a new sense of self-acceptance and inner peace.

So changed am I that my close friends have commented on the difference. Elaine, who had not seen me for a year, remarked, "Brenda, during the first few minutes after you walked into my kitchen, I knew you were different. That old restlessness is gone."

What has happened? God has brought me to the place where I now know that my worth is grounded in Him and in His love for me. He has reaffirmed the value of the mothering I give my children, and He is ever healing old, forgotten wounds.

And my identity—that burden of the modern era? As C. S. Lewis says so well on the last page of *Mere Christianity*, only Christ can tell us who we are. He alone gives us our real personalities when we cease to look for ourselves and give our lives to Him. But we must go to Jesus seeking Him and His life, not our own:

> As long as your own personality is what you are bothering about you are not going to Him at all. The very first step is to try to forget about the self altogether. Your real, new self (which is Christ's and also yours just because it is His) will not come as long as you are looking for it. It will come when you are looking for Him.[1]

There is no other way to find one's identity and personal fulfillment.

Once when I spoke on mothering to a group of doctors' wives, one woman objected vehemently to my conclusion. "Don't tell me about that 'born again' stuff," she said. "I am getting a degree in sociology, and I want to hear about real solutions for our culture's problems. Tell me how to find personal peace in the real world where kids get involved with sex and drugs and where husbands are immersed in careers." As I listened to this woman's anger and frustration, I knew that I could offer her no answer for personal peace apart from Christianity.

Not only are we unable to find personal peace apart from Jesus, but we are also unable to find true joy. We think just the opposite as we approach adulthood. Some of us believe that marriage or children or the beautiful house will fill up all the emptiness. But somehow nothing does. I spoke to an articulate, wealthy woman recently who had, only weeks before, tried to commit suicide. Possessing status and the world's goods, this woman still wanted to die.

Others of us go another route and believe that if we

have a career or are more glamorous or if we have fame and fortune then we will touch lives and eradicate the feelings of inner emptiness. "You cannot be too rich or too thin," we are told. But as we pursue this idea and attempt to tighten the flabby thighs or write the best seller, word comes that all is not well with the rich and famous. And so we sigh and resign ourselves to impoverished lives, not realizing that apart from Jesus, we will never find that all-too-elusive happiness.

Who are the happy, joyful people who walk the earth? Cheryl Tiegs or Farrah Fawcett, Johnny Carson or Phil Donahue? The most joyous men and women who have ever lived are, I believe, found in the ranks of the saints. Few have experienced the joy of Francis of Assisi as he walked through the snow of Italy's mountains barefoot, nursed lepers, or rebuilt the church at Portiuncula with his own hands. His joy was so contagious that the sons of Assissi's wealthy families flocked to the fields to join him, living in huts as brothers.

Or take the modern, uncanonized saint, Mother Teresa of Calcutta, who in early 1980 was given the Nobel Peace Prize. Who has not been touched by the beauty of this woman's life? As we read of her ministrations to the dying, the deserted babies often found in dustbins, or the lepers, we know that Jesus is alive today. He is alive and well in the person and the smile of Mother Teresa.

In *Something Beautiful for God,* Mother Teresa tells author Malcolm Muggeridge that she is a happy woman. Happiness to her means being with God in the present:

> loving as he loves,
> helping as he helps,
> giving as he gives,
> serving as he serves,
> rescuing as he rescues,
> being with him twenty-four hours,
> touching him in his distressing disguise.[2]

Not only is Mother Teresa joyous in her daily life, but the sisters who work with her are also filled with joy. Joy, in fact, is one of the hallmarks of the work done by the Sisters of Charity. Without joy, states Mother Teresa, they would not be serving Christ but would be engaged in social work. As with Saint Francis, this joy has attracted many women from upper-middle-class families who have renounced a comfortable existence for a demanding, yet fulfilling life of serving others.

According to Muggeridge, Mother Teresa has no problem with her identity.

> There is much talk today about discovering an identity as though it were something to be looked for, like winning a number in a lottery; then, once found, to be hoarded and treasured. Actually . . . the more it is spent the richer it becomes. So, with Mother Teresa, in effacing herself, she becomes herself. I never met anyone more memorable.[3]

But we are not Saint Francis or Mother Teresa, you say. Nor are we like the New Jersey mother Joanne Sheptock who, with her husband Rudy, parents twenty-nine children, all of whom are adopted. Several, like little John, who has no arms, are handicapped. Others have come to Rudy and Joanne from foster home situations only to find in their nineteen-room house in Peapack their first real home. Rudy, who works with a school system as maintenance supervisor, does not earn nearly enough to fund the needs of his large family. Their secret? Both are committed Christians who have discovered that as they open their hearts and home to each new child God sends, He provides all they need.

No, we may not be Saint Francis, Mother Teresa, or Joanne or Rudy Sheptock, but we can learn from their lives. They serve as lights in an increasingly dark world. Go, they say, to Jesus. Once there, relinquish your life and all the wrong ideas you cherish about yourself, knowing full well that you do not know what will ultimately make you happy. Nor do you have any idea of what your life could accomplish.

And in the process of relinquishing your life, you will become an original.

> Sameness is to be found most among the most "natural" men, not among those who surrender to Christ. How monotonously alike all the great tyrants and conquerors have been: how gloriously different are the saints.[4]

Joanne Sheptock is not patterned after Mother Teresa, and no one will ever become a Francis II. Though there have been numerous Teresas, all have been unique. And who will ever write like C. S. Lewis to touch the hearts and minds of the twentieth century?

The saints are, quite simply, those who give their complete selves to Jesus. Because of the totality of their commitment, they reach a level of human development unknown to most. While many strain to run, they soar.

As we give our complete selves to Jesus, as we live as saints, we will then discover that our children and husbands are no deterrent to the fulfilled life. Rather, they fit hand and glove with our own needs to love, belong, and nurture. Once our questing has led us to Christ, we then know that our lives will not narrow as our children mature; on the contrary, God will fill every nook and cranny with meaning and purpose. Along the way we will find that we are happiest—gloriously, deeply happy—when we are giving love to others.

And who knows what we may become?

WHERE HAVE ALL THE MOTHERS GONE?

[1]C. S. Lewis, *Mere Christianity* (Great Britain: Fonatana Books, 1952), p. 188.
[2]Malcolm Muggeridge, *Something Beautiful for God* (New York: Doubleday and Co., Inc., 1971), p. 50.
[3]Ibid., p. 14.
[4]Lewis, *Mere Christianity*, pp. 187–88.